D1568510

How To Screw Up Your Kids

Blended Families, Blendered Style

Pamela Fagan Hutchins

How To Screw Up Your Kids

SkipJack Publishing books may be purchased for educational, business, or sales promotional use. For information, please write: Sales, SkipJack Publishing, P.O.B. 31160 Houston, TX 77231.

First U.S. Edition
Hutchins, Pamela Fagan
How To Screw Up Your Kids /by Pamela Fagan Hutchins
ISBN-13: 978-0-9882348-3-3 (SkipJack Publishing)

To "Liz," for making the middle look so easy, when
I know it wasn't.

Acknowledgments

Huge thanks to my editor Meghan Pinson, who managed to keep my ego intact without sacrificing her editorial integrity. Thanks of generous proportions to my writing group, without whose encouragement and critiques I would not be publishing this book. Love and thanks to Thomas, Marie, and Liz for letting me into their lives, and to them as well as to Clark and Susanne for enriching mine. And thanks to the power of infinity to my husband Eric, for his co-parenting, patience, and support.

Thanks also to Alex Dumetriscu and Heidi Dorey for fabulous cover art. The photography credits go to Eric and me.

Other Books by the Author

The Clark Kent Chronicles: A Mother's Tale Of Life With Her ADHD/Asperger's Son, SkipJack Publishing

Hot Flashes And Half Ironmans: Middle-Aged Endurance Athletics Meets the Hormonally Challenged, SkipJack Pub.

Love Gone Viral: Couples Who Make You Wanna Puke, And How To Be Part Of One, SkipJack Publishing

Saving Grace, SkipJack Publishing

Puppalicious And Beyond: Life Outside The Center Of The Universe, SkipJack Publishing

Easy To Love, But Hard To Raise (anthology), DRT Press, edited by Kay Marner & Adrienne Ehlert Bashista

Easy To Love, But Hard To Teach (anthology), DRT Press, edited by Kay Marner & Adrienne Ehlert Bashista

Ghosts! (anthology), Aakenbaaken & Kent, edited by Lynne Gregg & Julian Kindred

Prevent Workplace Harassment, Prentice Hall, with the Employment Practices Solutions attorneys

Table of Contents

DESPITE OUR BEST EFFORTS

It's not that we didn't try to screw this parenting thing up. By all rights, we should have. We did everything that we possibly could that we weren't supposed to do. We gave them refined sugar when they were babies, didn't enforce nap times, spoiled them with expensive and unnecessary gifts. We said yes when we should have said no. We said no when we should have said yes. Our swear jar was always full.

Oh, yeah. And we were one of those "blended families" — you know the kind, the ones with broken homes, divorces, stepparents and complex custody arrangements. Those people. The ones other parents are leery of, like divorce is a communicable disease or something. Who knows? Maybe it is. My own parents even told me once that I had made my children a statistic by choosing to divorce their father. That I had created an at-risk home environment for them.

Me? Perpetual overachiever, business owner, attorney, former cheerleader and high school beauty queen? The one who's never even smoked a cigarette, much less done drugs? My husband? Well, he's the more likely candidate for an at-risk homemaker. Surfer, bass player, triathlon enthusiast. Oh yeah, and chemical engineer and former officer of a ten-billion-dollar company — but you know how those rock-n-rollers are. We probably teeter somewhere between the Bundys and the Cleavers.

But there we were, watching yet another of our kids cross yet another stage for yet another diploma, with honors, with accolades, with activities — with college scholarships, no less. Yeah, I know, yadda yadda yap. There we were, cheering as the announcer called Liz's name. Three of her four siblings rose to clap, too. The fourth one, Thomas, couldn't make it because he was doing time in the state penitentiary in Florida. (Just kidding. He had to work. At a job. That paid him and provided benefits.)

We tried our best to screw it up. We had the perfect formula. But we didn't — not even close. Somehow two losers at their respective Round Ones in love and family unity got it close to perfect on Round

Two. By our standards, anyway. Because we didn't give a good goldarnit about anyone else's.

What's more? We got it right on purpose. We made a plan, and we executed the plan. And it worked. After all that effort to screw things up, after the people in our lives who loved us most wrung their hands and whispered behind our backs (and those who didn't love us chortled in anticipation of our certain failure), we went out and done good.

Now, I'm no expert on child rearing (although I've had lots of practice), but I am an expert in helping grownups play nice and behave at work. How annoying is that? I know. I'm a scary hybrid of employment attorney and human resources professional, blended together to create a problem-solving HR consultant. And from where I sat, our blended household—or blendered family, as we call it— looked a lot like a dysfunctional workplace in our early days.

Or a little warren of guinea pigs on which I could conduct my own version of animal testing.

The HR principles I applied at work were, in theory, principles for humans, humans anywhere. Blendering occurs in workplaces when a leadership team gets a couple of new members, and it happens in a home with kids from different families of origins.

HR principles = people principles = *blendering* principles. Right? That was my theory, anyway.

Statistics tell me that you, dear reader, are or will be in similar straits: divorced, starting over, trying to make it work. If you've already been there and done that, I hope you've disappointed all your naysayers, too. You'll enjoy this book all the more as you relate to the pains and the joys of blended families. But if you're on the cusp of what feels like an express train descending into hell and wondering how to buy a ticket back, I can help you.

Really.

Okay, probably.

If not probably, then quite possibly.

At the very least, maybe I can say I warned you, or made you laugh. It's a crazy and unpredictable ride, but the destination is worth it.

HOW DID THE BRADYS DO IT?

Blendering Principle #1: It's hard to get anywhere if you don't know where you're going.

Most of the members of my generation know all we need to know about blended families from the Brady Bunch, right?

Not.

Please, folks. That was just a sappy television show, and didn't Florence Henderson have an affair IRL[1] with one of the TV sons? Sounds a lot like incest to me. We clearly need a new set of role models, yet I'd be vacationing in Fiji right now if I had a nickel for

---

[1] In real life.

every time someone said to me, "Oh! You're just like the Brady Bunch!"

The Bradys wove their magic through engaging scripts and clever sets, cute young actors and the star power of Florence Henderson. Eric and I didn't have those crutches to lean on. Neither will you.

Real blended families start with two adults who want to pledge their troth, which in English means they want to marry. Or at least cohabitate with commitment. Oh, hell, maybe not even that. But that conundrum brings us to the genesis of our blended family success, and IMHO[2], a critical element.

Each of our kids had already endured one familial breakup. Were we ready to provide them stability and an example of enduring love? If not, why would we knowingly put them through sure trauma again? Nothing is certain in life, but Eric and I were all in. Not only were we all in, but we both had a consuming desire to demonstrate to our children the type of relationship we dreamed of for them, and neither of us felt like we had done so in our past lives. Scratch that. We absolutely *knew* we had not done so in our past lives.

---

[2] In my humble opinion. Seriously, folks, get with the pop culture.

So, we were madly in love and promised forever. Believed forever. Were confident in forever.

Still, this left a lot up to chance.

Pretend for a second that you married a touchy-feely HR consultant. Imagine that she had a penchant for things like mission, vision, and values statements. Picture her love of goal-setting and accountability. Some of you have mentally drawn up your divorce papers already.

Eric didn't. He and I created a relationship operating agreement (ROA) for ourselves as a couple. I may or may not have promised years of sexual favors to secure his participation, but his attitude about the project was good. Now, this isn't a relationship book. Well, it is, in a way. It is a book about our relationships with our children within a blended family. But it is not a couples' relationship book, so I'll spare you the gory details behind the ROA.

While we entered into our ROA to make our great relationship stronger, we did so knowing it would set the framework for co-parenting. Why? Because our kids were the most important things to each of us, besides one another. And since most second marriages break down over issues of stepparenting, money, or sex. Hell, many first marriages crash and burn on those issues. We had less than ideal co-parenting relationships with our exes, for sure.

So here's how our ROA looks:

Our (Exceptionally Wonderful) Marriage
Mantra: Make it all small stuff.

Our relationship's purpose is to create a loving, nurturing, safe environment that enables us to
- make a positive, joyful difference in each other's lives,
- respect each other's needs and differences,
- encourage each other's spiritual, emotional, and physical needs and development,
- practice caring, open communication,
- role-model loving relationships to our children, and
- work as partners when we parent and make major decisions.

Because we recognize that life is not always about the incredible highs, we are committed to these strategies:
- Stop, breathe, and be calm.
- Allow ourselves to cherish and be cherished.

- Be positive. Assume a positive intent and give a positive response. Speak your mind as positively as possible.
- Be reasonable. Am I being oversensitive? Am I dragging my own issues in unnecessarily?
- Be considerate. Is there anything to gain from what I am about to say? Is this the right time to say it?
- Be respectful. Don't mope, don't name-call, don't yell, don't be sarcastic.
- Be open. Explain your intent.
- Be present. Don't walk away, physically or emotionally.
- Be aware of time and energy. After 60 minutes, stop talking. Schedule another conversation for 24 hours later if there's no resolution.
- Make it safe to cry "calf rope."
- *Be* it. Do the behaviors you're seeking in each other within an hour of the first conversation.
- Be loving. Don't go to bed angry or with things unresolved.

He asks of her:
- Trust and have faith that I love you, enough that we don't have to solve everything the second it happens.
- Assume a positive intent.
- Listen, don't interrupt.
- Don't be sarcastic.

She asks of him:
- Come back to me faster and don't drag things out, because I need you.
- Speak your mind assertively, and don't be sarcastic.
- Don't assume the actions I take are always because of you.
- Assume a positive intent.

We didn't get this smart on our own. Both of us were trained to draft this type of agreement in our work lives, one of us more than the other. I specialize in working with hyper-competitive, confident-bordering-on-egomaniacal executives who are somewhat lacking in people skills, so I've spent years mediating, soothing, recalibrating, and at times walloping high-level business people into line. One of the best tools to get all the warring co-workers from different backgrounds to reach détente is an operating agreement. Even better? An operating agreement grounded in shared values, vision, and mission.

This worked so well for me with one of my problem executives that we ended up married. In fact, you just read our operating agreement.

Blendering Principle #2: Your mom was almost right: Do unto others as *they* would have done unto them.

So we addressed parenting, but more importantly, we addressed how we would handle ourselves in situations of higher stress and greater conflict. All of our commitments about behavior applied equally to the parenting context. Now, when a parent/stepparent decision point arose, we could act in accordance with pre-agreed principles.

Or we could try.

Execution got a little sloppy at times. When it did, we always had the agreement to return to, a touchstone, a refocusing point, a document which reminded us that for all we didn't agree on, there was oh-so-much-more that we did.

We filtered our day-to-day co-parenting decisions through this model. Chores, allowances, length of skirts, cell phones — you name it, we used it. Even better, we used it when we designed our family structure and plan. Did I mention I believe in planning? I believe in plans. And I believe in modifying the plan within the context of agreed principles when new circumstances arise. We got the chance for a lot of planning and re-planning, right from the start.

When Eric and I first married, his eldest son Thomas had graduated from college and had a real job, Eric's middle daughter Marie was entering college in the South, and his youngest daughter Liz lived with her mother on the East Coast. My Susanne was in elementary school, and my ADHD son Clark was in middle school; they split their time between their father and me. Our original parenting plan called for the two youngest kids to live mostly with us, for Liz to visit frequently, and for us to see Marie and Thomas as often as possible.

We envisioned all of our children, and someday their children, in our home as frequently as we could get them there. We bought a house in a great school district in Houston, with a veritable dormitory of four bedrooms upstairs and our master bedroom on the far side of the downstairs—because we love our kids even more from a distance. And how could we resist this house? It has a lush back yard with a three-level pond full of fat goldfish and koi that reminds us of the home we left behind on St. Croix in the U.S. Virgin Islands.

Just as this is not a book about couples' relationships, it is also not a book about divorce or custody battles. I could dish on those, but I won't, because even though I've changed the names of all parties in this little tome to protect the innocent[3], some things should and will remain private. They were painful. Isn't that the case in all divorces? You don't divorce because the relationship exceeded your expectations. You don't divvy up with a light heart the time you will spend with children you cherish. Most of you don't, anyway, and we sure didn't.

So, for whatever reason, within four months of "I do," Liz had taken up primary residence with us in Texas, and a year later Marie transferred to a university two hours away. I had never pictured myself taking a role of such primacy with two teenage stepdaughters. Teenage girls get a bad rap for good reason. It's not the easiest time in their lives, or the easiest time for the people that love them, even with great girls like Liz and Marie. Yet this new arrange-

---

[3] Criteria that requires Eric and me to use our real names.

ment fit the model we envisioned. We just needed to flex. A lot.

I held onto my husband's hand for dear life and sucked in one deep, cleansing breath after another. We could do this. I could do this. We would have no regrets or remorse, we would give our kids the best we could, and be damn happy doing it. Yeah!

And so, very carefully and very cautiously, we began to blender.

BLENDERING

Blendering Principle #3: Culture is everything.

Family culture evolves slowly, but it eventually becomes so ingrained that even though most of the time we take it for granted, we will go to battle over it in a heartbeat.

And at our house, sometimes we do. It is who we are. We're a feisty group, in a good way. Call it self-confidence. So, what happens when who we are — the family structure we've always had — changes? What survives, what dies, and what is reborn? Our kids had a lot of good stuff they wanted to hang on to: summer vacations in Maine for his kids, Christmas in New Mexico for mine, Thanksgiving dinner menus, birthday breakfasts of half-baked chocolate chip pancakes for his girls, rabid devotion to Texas A&M football in my house.

Eric and I faced a restructuring challenge when his then-thirteen-year-old daughter Liz moved in with us, Clark (11) and Susanne (9). We had navigated the "stepsiblings living in separate houses" issue before, and while that was not without its perils, the boats had sailed on relatively smooth waters. Our main issue until the blender event was hurt feelings over time each parent spent with non-birth kids.

And then we blendered. With that plan I mentioned earlier. And a schedule. Preceded by research. (My poor husband, I know.) But what we wanted to co-create was too important to leave to chance.

We had just moved to Houston from the Caribbean, so we found ourselves with three friendless kids newly thrown together in the house for a long summer of empty days with only me — I work from home — to shepherd them. Oh yeah, and we were broke. Zero cash, flat-out broke. We weren't going to be able to throw expensive days at Schlitterbahn Water Park at this problem.

Our plan involved holding themed family events on the cheap each night of the week. Monday, ping-pong. Tuesday, board games. Wednesday, movies. Thursday, kids cook. Friday, swim night. Saturday, family night out (on a strict budget).

We had a rotation for which kid got to choose the details; which movie, which board game, the menu, what our night out would be. We kept up this schedule all summer and some vestiges remain, years later.

It was powerfully effective. Why?

Because everything we did, we did as a family. And we made memories. We did not sit around and whine about what to do; we were active. We established a pattern that the kids looked forward to repeating. We honored each other's choices, even when we hated them. Although we weren't above bartering with Clark to try to get out of another game of Risk on game night.

Now, this blender summer was not without tears. It wasn't without tense moments, angry Facebook statuses (woopsie), and one-on-one conversations between parent and child. We expected that. It was okay. We had kids with big emotions that we were trying to move from fear and hurt into love and faith. Each of the kids worked with a counselor at various points in the process, to mixed but generally positive results. We found a great church where Liz made friends and joined the choir.

And we gently evolved those one-on-one parent-child conversations into parent-parent-child as the weeks went on. We partnered, as we had agreed. It was uncomfortable at times. But we were becoming *real*. Like a family. So we kept up with the plan.

We did other bonding silliness. At the end of the summer, we paid for dinner for five at P.F. Chang's with the parental contributions to the $1 swear jar. I told my kids they should thank me for finding a stepfather whose colorful language paid off so well. We paid for one month's water bill with the kids' deposits into the $1 turn-off-the-lights jar. We doled out chores on a rotating schedule because nobody wanted to clean up dog poop three weeks in a row during the Houston summer. We enacted a strict oldest-to-youngest rule to avoid constant battles and fears of favoritism, like who got to ride shotgun. Poor Susanne never got to sit in the front seat. She's still claiming abuse.

Another tradition we kicked off that first summer was picking up tacky souvenirs when we traveled. Not just any old tacky souvenirs, but odd, gaudy and large objects that received a place of honor in our living room display. We made our first purchase the day before our wedding; we bought a jeweled wire gecko—a hideously beautiful creature. On a weekend trip to Brenham, Texas, in July of that first summer, the kids added Lenny, a wood and tin armadillo. This tradition thrives still. Our family treasures include a steel cowboy, a log grizzly bear, a ceramic dancing hula cat, and many more gauche objets d'art.

By August, we decided our fledgling relationships were ready to leave the nest; we attempted a two-week migration from Houston to Maine and back with the five of us in the Suburban. The destination was key. As the latest comer into the blended household, we wanted Liz to have the opportunity to introduce her new siblings to a special Hutchins place. Some of her best memories were from her grandparents' cabin on Lake Mooselookmeguntic.

So Maine it would be.

IT'S THE MAINE THING.

Every family has its special place. Mine growing up was my grandparents' farm in Stephenville, Texas. We used to fly there in my grandfather's Cessna, with my brother and me sitting with rope "seatbelts" in the seatless space where seats should go. We landed on the dirt strip Grandpa Joe built himself. I loved slopping the pigs, making home-made hand-churned ice cream, picking figs from the tree in the backyard, and gathering the chicken eggs. But that was my past. My husband, Thomas, Marie, and Liz had quite a different experience.

For them, it all dated back to around 1970, when a remarkable family came upon a remarkable lake called Mooselookmeguntic in northwest Maine. Legend has it that the lake was named for an Indian who rattled that string of syllables while describing his near-death experience involving a moose and a misfiring gun. The Hutchinses were driving their camper inland from the coast of Maine with no particular destination when they came upon the beautiful area of Mooselook, near Oquossoc (which is near Rangeley, which is near nothing in particular). They saw signs advertising lakefront lots for sale— only $700—and before you knew it, the Cruzans from St. Croix, U.S. Virgin Islands, had themselves a steep, rocky, heavily forested piece of usually-frozen heaven.

For the next few summers, Eric's parents brought their three young boys up to Maine, where they camped across the street from the new house they were building together. Larry was a builder, and sometimes work would take him back to St. Croix, and Beth would be left alone with her boisterous sons for weeks on end. Mom and sons roughed it alone with a station wagon and a canvas tent. They fended off mosquitoes the size of their heads. Moose and bear visited their campsite. And they had to endure the cold, cold rain.

On one such solo parenting expedition, Beth kept a list of all her sons' transgressions. She wrote that one was "blowing his nose without the aid of a handkerchief." She vividly recounted geckos from the islands getting loose on the airplane on the way to Maine; those that made it didn't last long, and the sight of lizard skeletons, so familiar in the islands, became a part of the Maine landscape as well. Beth said she once looked up from making pancakes to see a lizard dangling lifeless from the loft above her head on its leash-cum-accidental-noose.

When the time came to erect their A-frame, Larry enlisted the help of his wife and sons, tying ropes around people and trees as they set up the supports (without killing any small children). There were many mishaps, but none critical, the worst of which was when Larry referred to Beth as his wench; he says he meant it in building terms. Anyway, a house was built, and then came the gravy years.

What could be a better life than winters in St. Croix and summers in Maine? Miniature golf courses built through the forest . . . fishing and water skiing . . . picnicking on Blueberry Island . . . clandestine body surfing at Upper Dam . . . walking home in the dark from dinners with lifelong friends. An overly sure of himself neighbor nearly hydroplaning into their dock . . . and later waterskiing a little too far onto the beach and catapulting himself over his audience and their bonfire . . . accidentally towing a boat trailer several miles underwater behind their boat (very, very slowly) . . . saving up all summer to spend their hoarded dollars at the local auction, only to discover they'd bought left- instead of right-handed golf clubs . . . lifting weights made of logs, like the Flintstones. Awesomesauce, totally.

The years passed and the sons grew up. They visited less frequently. The grownup boys' jobs did not permit them the flexibility their father once had to bring their families to their boyhood summer paradise.

Still, the cabin became the favorite place of the next generation, and the grandchildren, including Thomas, Marie, and Liz, enjoyed the same type of adventures as their dad. Years passed. Boathouses, docks, and decks were added. Boats came, boats died, boats went.

This was a place of tradition, of family love; a very special place to the Hutchins. And then came the summer of 2007, when Liz and Eric shared the Mooselook cabin with Clark, Susanne, and me. The time came for us to make new memories in our own way, together.

Trippin' the Light Fantastic

Our lean family finances dictated that we make the trip by car rather than plane, and we had just the right vehicle. Our 2000 Chevy Suburban was in great shape, but not so new that we would stress out about the dust and dings of a long road trip. Eric's co-worker lent us a rooftop carrier, so even with five occupants, the Suburban would be roomy enough that the kids would have to stretch to hit each other. It boasted plenty of outlets for car chargers and adaptors, too, a must with multiple laptops and DVDs players in tow. We made music CDs and checked out audiobooks and DVDs from the library. We even splurged on the final Harry Potter audio-book.

And I put together a plan, over the eyerolls of my four travelling companions, a plan that was to foreshadow every future jaunt of our blended family. A new family tradition, if you will. I plotted our trip carefully with aggressive daily mileage goals mandated by prepaid hotels at our interim destinations. I set and met a cap of an average of $100 per night for the five of us, all-inclusive with continental breakfasts. I'm a budgeting rock star. This meant Clark slept on an air mattress and Liz and Susanne shared a bed, but no one complained. At least not very loudly.

Blendering Principle #4: Live your plan.

We packed in a rather unorthodox fashion that required way more preplanning than our kids were used to, in day bags that we identified by city, wearer, and date. Instead of bringing suitcases into the hotels, we each brought in a plastic bag, and I brought in a large family bathroom bag. The next morning, our dirties went into the plastic bags and were exchanged into the designated dirties suitcase. The stress of frequently changing hotels was lots lower (for me) without toting in and pawing through too many suitcases, and repacking frantically strewn clothing every morning.

Isn't this how everyone does their family trips??

Maybe not. But don't tell our kids that, because they accepted it. Came to expect it. Maybe even secretly enjoyed all the pre-work, like a prequel to the adventure.

Eric and I informed our beloved offspring on day one that we would strictly enforce a No Bickering rule. We also said we would rotate through the kids in age order each time a decision-making opportunity came up.

By the end of day one, Clark and Susanne were ousted from the Suburban and walked along a small-town sidewalk for a few hundred yards while deciding whether they would like to ride in the car without fighting. In 5,000 miles, we only had to do this twice; the second time was on a dirt road in Maine. That time, they straightened up even quicker. Thank you, giant bloodsucking mosquitoes.

Our kids had previously lived a spoiled and happy life. On this trip, we carried our food and beverages with us, pre-purchased at Sam's. The budget—which I printed out, carried with us, and consulted and quoted from annoyingly on a regular basis—permitted very little eating out. Rest stops were for gas and bathroom only, and we all worked together to find the cheapest gas. Whining was minimal, and complaints about the turkey sandwiches were whispered from the backseat and accompanied by giggles.

Our biggest driving challenge was that the kids and I had the gas and bathroom stops down to a science, but hadn't anticipated the impact Eric would have on our anticipated pit stop time. We spent a lot of time standing outside the men's restroom waiting for him to rejoin us. The kids became more and more brutal as the trip progressed, until Eric finally just handed us the keys as soon as we pulled to a stop and ran to the bathroom as the taunts rang out behind him. There's really nothing like poo jokes to bring a family together.

Liz designated herself the official trip historian. She kept a notebook like a reporter and constantly flipped through, adding quotes, favorite things, funny events, and general commentary. She recorded such immortal lines as Clark's "My life goal is to be a dork" and "Let's go see *Harry Potter and the Butt of the Monkey*." No, we still don't understand that last one.

Our plan was to drive to Auburn on day one to visit Eric's oldest daughter Marie. As on each of the next thirteen days, we stopped at every state line (twenty-eight in all) and took a photo; Eric and I alternated as photographer, and Lenny our pet armadillo appeared in every picture. If someone was asleep, we woke their lazy butt up and dragged them out of the Suburban anyway.

Marie seemed to really enjoy our visit for the first hour or so. The kids adored being with her. She was not swayed by our pleas for her to join us on the rest of the trip, though, and I swear I heard her whoop with joy when we all were finally out of her hair.

Our next marquee stop was Niagara Falls. Eric and Liz had both visited it before, but Clark, Susanne, and I were neophytes. We had our first ugly mood swing (Clark), but the splendor of the falls was so amazing that we were able to block it (him) out. We got drenched on the Maid of the Mist, and re-drenched for good measure at Cave of the Winds.

Thirty-six hours later, we made it to Mooselook. Eric and Liz had bubbled over with memories for the last two hundred miles, and we spent the next five days making new ones of our own.

The kids and Eric fished for hours every day and argued for months over who caught what. We ate dinners on the deck with handpicked blue lupine centerpieces. We picnicked on Student's and Blueberry Islands. Liz wakeboarded, I stayed out of the freezing water, and Eric spent far too much time in it fixing boats.

We had saved all our laundry to do in Maine, but the water system failed. Not only did we end up with dirty clothes, but we had to make innumerable trips down to the lake with buckets so we could flush toilets and wash dishes—a lot less hard work than Beth and the gang endured thirty-five years ago, so we didn't mind, although we did tone up our glutes. We were all equally stinky due to our aversion to bathing in freezing lake water, but Mooselook had us crazy in love, and toting water was just part of its charm.

A thousand memories made in a very short period of time left everyone wanting more, but the road home stretched before us and our jobs beckoned. On the way back, we swung through New York and visited Ellis and Liberty Islands, finding several of Beth's ancestors in the records on Ellis. We capped the day by losing our keys to the Suburban and the car-top carrier, necessitating our meeting a very nice and high-priced locksmith named Gino.

We stopped in Washington, D.C., and Eric took the kids for a whirlwind tour of the memorials and museums while I took a good, long nap. While they were out, Eric ended up paying another locksmith to get the keys out of the car, where he'd locked them. He swore the kids to secrecy on the second key fiasco, and Liz held her tongue for a whole twenty-four hours before spilling the truth over dinner.

Finally, we scurried down to Jacksonville, Florida, to see Beth and Larry and share with them how grateful we were that thanks to their impetuously perfect decision to buy their $700 lakefront lot, and thanks even more to their years of hard work, the cabin at Mooselook still existed for everyone to enjoy. And to nurture our blossoming family.

The whole time we were in Maine, we searched for the perfect tacky travel souvenir. Our hearts longed for a moose, but none we saw were just right. So, when we got home, Liz—the one we had so worried about blendering into our new tribe—built a wobbly-legged moose out of scrap lumber and toolbox odds and ends. And she put together a massive scrapbook of the trip.

We logged five thousand miles, twenty-eight states, and fourteen days together in that Suburban. By the time we got home, Mooselook had three more devoted fans, and a happy thirteen-year-old girl who had the fun of sharing it all with us.

Success.

SPEED BUMPS IN THE
YELLOW BRICK ROAD

After that idyllic trip to Maine, off we rode in our jeweled carriage down the yellow brick road into the golden sunset.

Riiiiggghhhhtt.

There were bumps in those yellow bricks. Some the size of a Sherman tank. But when it came to establishing culture and tradition, most of them were more Volkswagen bug-sized. Not quite insubstantial, but smallish.

Take holidays, for example. Most custody arrangements provide for holiday rotations. Mine did. My husband's didn't.

Since Eric got Liz nearly full time, she spent holidays with her mother, and his older two kids, Thomas and Marie, followed suit. Christmas without his kids makes Eric sad, as you can imagine. This made it harder for us to establish traditions around the holidays as a blendered family, although we did celebrate together, albeit early.

Liz spent most of the summer holidays with her mom, too, so after that one fantastic Maine trip, there were no more summer vacations of any length. It's a bummer, but we made do by cramming in three-day weekends when we could, with jaunts to my parents' small ranch and to a mountain cabin in New Mexico as the favorites.

Some traditions survived the transition, although not always as blended occasions. Maine, we did together. But my kids have kept up their lifelong tradition of a small-town peach and melon festival without their stepsiblings. Eric still makes the disgusting half-baked chocolate chip pancakes and waffles that his kids have always loved but none of the rest of us can stand. And, of course, each set of kids has traditions that they maintain with their other parents. My kids trek to Steamboat each year with their father, for example, while Eric's offspring love gathering to eat their mom's famous lasagna.

The traditions of one family of origin crash into the traditions of the other with a loud bang from time to time. The most dramatic culture clash we experienced involved Christmas cards.

In my birth family, sending holiday cards is a BIG DEAL. We are from the South, y'all. In our part of the world, you start planning for the perfect photo for *next* Christmas on December 26th. You struggle to write an obnoxious family letter that is only one page, and usually give up and write three to four pages. Your mailing list is the size of the Yellow Pages. When the holiday season arrives, the best moment of each day is when the mail comes and you get to dive into the day's offerings of cards! letters! photos! You display them all over the house — sometimes on special artsy-craftsy bulletin boards in the shape of Christmas trees or festively wrapped holiday gifts. You read them over, and over, and over. Even if you don't talk to these people all year and your only remaining contact is the cards, you hang on every word of the letters and read them aloud to your spouse and kids.

That's my family. Not my husband's. And his older kids Thomas and Marie did not have a frame of reference for my family's tradition at all. They thought that participation in a family holiday photo with their father would hurt their mother's feelings, and they refused to do it. At first, it really hurt our feelings. Tempers flared, harsh words were exchanged. Over time, though, Eric and I understood the culture gap, and the last thing we wanted ever to do was make any of the kids feel they had to choose between the feelings of one parent over another. Liz didn't mind, though—anything that entailed a picture with her in it was bound to be awesome.

Blendering Principle #5: Pick your battles very carefully.

Anyway, I developed a family culture blendering rule. Most things aren't important enough to battle over. But Christmas cards are! I wouldn't include a picture of anyone that didn't want to be in it, but I would not stop doing photos for cards or pretend that my family did not now include more wonderful people than it had before. We adopted an inclusion rule for photo cards of only those "living in the household," and this has been an acceptable compromise. Here's an example:

If you had asked me at the age of twenty-two whether I wanted a failed first marriage and the responsibility for blendering a family in my final marriage, I would have cringed and said, "Hell no!" But I would not trade any of our five kids, beautiful and perfect in part because of who their parents are, nor would I trade the opportunity to have them all in my life just to have skipped the hard parts.

And I certainly would not have wanted to miss out on this incredible journey that Eric and I have traveled together, combining the worlds and traditions of these young people until that wonderful moment when you hear all of them fighting and yelling at each other without respect to who is related to whom, and you say to each other, "Ah, at last, we've done it. Everything is just perfect."

"Now, Susanne, quit yelling at your stepsister, and stay on your own side of the back seat."

I AIN'T NO FREAKIN' NURTURER.

So there we were, all blendered and chock-a-full of new memories and traditions, according to plan. Even before that, though, we'd had, or rather, *I'd* had a revelation. A revelation that made all the difference for me. Maybe for all of us.

Flashback to the islands, pre-move to Texas:

My earthy yang-to-my-yin friend Valerie sat across from Eric, Marie, and me at a tiny patio table at a now-defunct but then-fabulous French restaurant called Le St. Tropez. Before her, she held the numerology reports she had done on Eric, Marie, and me in honor of our upcoming move.

I didn't know much about numerology, but I do believe in fate, and in opening up to the answers that are out there. It makes perfect sense to me that different cultures have different ways of listening.

My culture taught me to listen through prayer. Numerology teaches the relation between numbers and living things. I could accept that people find comfort and truth in this ancient practice; I didn't entirely discount it, but I didn't exactly believe in it. I tried to keep an open mind.

Valerie started with Eric. "My results for Eric show him as a conqueror, someone strong and powerful and dominant."

I could definitely see that in him, so her work gained a little credibility. I was eager to hear about me, but I already knew I would also be a powerful, dominant conqueror

"I get the same result for Marie," Valerie said.

Oh, definitely, I could see that, too. Even at barely eighteen, Marie kicked some serious butt.

"For you, Pamela, I get nurturer, supporter, and helper," Valerie continued.

The needle screeched off the side of the vinyl record and the breezy soundtrack in my head came to a halt.

Me, a NURTURER? Absolutely not. My husband shifted around in his chair and snorted. He knew what was coming.

All my life I had rebelled against what I perceived as a submissive role. I flunked home economics in middle school (the same year I was salutatorian). I fought bitterly with my parents over what I saw as their gender-differentiated treatment of my brother and me. I pursued a law degree. I declined to use the word "submit" in my first-wedding vows. I started a business, then later became an officer at an oil refining company. Sure, I married and had kids, but I was all sharp angles, hard edges, and blunt force: the General. Warm and nurturing? No way. Just ask my ex-husband.

"No, absolutely not. Untrue. Even if it is true, it isn't—because I don't want it to be. Do it again. I'm what they are," I said, gesturing to Marie and Eric.

Valerie assured me that the numbers don't lie.

"A bunch of occult nonsense," I protested.

I wasn't going to worry about it. But I did worry.

The next day, Valerie and I decided to test the numerology results with the I Ching, which was just as foreign to me as numerology. She explained that the I Ching is an age-old Chinese oracle; I would ask questions, and Valerie would divine the answers by tossing three coins to cast hexagrams. In the old days, instead of coins, the practitioners tossed yarrow stalks, whatever those are. The hexagrams were based on the concept of yin and yang.

It made no sense whatsoever to me, but I was pretty desperate to disprove the numerology report.

Valerie encouraged me to keep the question neutral. I should not ask it "Am I to be a Nurturer?" or "Am I to be a Conqueror?" as that might bias the results.

I had my question ready. "Where am I headed?" I whispered.

I started tossing the coins. Six times I tossed coins, six times she wrote results from bottom to top, creating my hexagram. Then she consulted her I Ching book. Her explanation was long. It involved "multiple moving lines" and "changing lines." She talked about present versus future lines. I pressed for an answer. She shushed me, explaining that she had to read everything to me and we'd soak it in together. Finally, though, she announced she had my answer: my primary hexagram was Grouping, which was often translated as "Holding Together."

I looked at the other hexagrams. I wanted the Great Power or the Biting Through. I wanted to be a Conqueror or a Victor. But that was not the answer from the coins.

We talked for a long time about finding my own meaning in the words of explanation in the I Ching, but when I left her house I was still chafing. Any fool could see it meant I was to be a nurturer.

Eric was not surprised by the answer I got from the I Ching. He reminded me that I had told him my greatest desire in our relationship was to soften myself for him, to be feminine, less controlling. I had said I didn't want to shove myself down his throat, and that I wanted to be able to accept romance, support, and love.

Maybe I wasn't at the point of complete acceptance yet, but my own soul called out to be a nurturer. Honestly, what was I fighting so hard for? My whole life I had defined my success and happiness by standards that did not include a category for nurturing; yet the inescapable reality was that I had not found happiness or success in a core relationship. I had failed at the one thing that mattered most to me.

Until now. Until I gave my heart to Eric and declared my desire to support and partner rather than dominate and control. I thought of all the personality-type tests I had taken over the years, and I knew there was great value in figuring out who you really are and adjusting to yourself, your situations, and to others, as opposed to forcing yourself into a life for someone you only think you are.

**Blendering Principle #6: Bloom like mad, no
matter where you are planted.**

Over the course of the next year or two, my path
was chosen for me, coins or no coins. My children
and my husband needed me. Eric's children needed
us. I did not resist (very hard, anyway). I let go. I
clung to the remnants of my professional life to the
extent that our family still needed my smaller-than-
before but still scale-tipping income, but not at the
expense of . . . well . . . nurturing. My fragile self-
esteem strengthened after an initial floundering free-
fall. I became visibly joyous, even radiant. I was not
the woman I once was; I was better.

My younger brother has always jokingly called
me a femi-nazi (he is a Marine, 'nuf said), so all you
strong, ambitious women, take clear note of my
meaning: This was not about subjugating myself to a
gender role, this was about accepting my own
personal fate, the one I had egotistically fought
against in pursuit of what my "self" thought it
wanted.

I had to overcome my own stereotypes and learn
that rather than being submissive in the sense of
weakness or neediness, a nurturer must be strong. As
a nurturer, I was a champion and a fighter, but only

on behalf of those most important to me. I did not lose my sense of self—the cliff-jumping warrior goddess—I simply changed my focus.

As a nurturer, I did ordinary extraordinary things. I worked on a Peter Pan costume for my son's school musical, took Liz to the dentist, talked Marie off a ledge about her job, worked on a résumé with Thomas, and helped Susanne address flagging grades, while coaching and encouraging my husband in the throes of his pre-speech jitters. I made sure everyone got to the right place at the right time with the right food and the right clothes, and turned off fifteen lights as I cleaned up the aftermath of the whirlwind.

I managed to cram in a client conference call while they were at school. In my humble opinion I was brilliant, and it still felt great, but my professional workload was deliberately modest. I can't help but bring that professional experience with me, though. My household suffers through the impact of the ROA Eric and I hung on the fridge (with little hearts on it, no less), one-on-one coaching sessions, and group conflict resolution meetings at the dining room table.

I fought the label and my edges stayed a little sharp, but Nurturer was the role I filled, and, for the first time in my adult life, I was fulfilled and at peace.

I don't know if there is anything to numerology or those silly coins, but I do know that whether by accident or accuracy, they were right, and I bow humbly to the hand that guides me.

My stepdad is my hero.

**Blendering Principle #7: Make your stories
legends with heroes and fire-breathing dragons.**

Once upon a time, we lived in a big house named
Estate Annaly on a hill in the rainforest on St. Croix.
Our place was remote, so we had need for security;
enter our six dogs, a Brady Bunch assortment like our

kids. Eric brought three: Jake, a cockermation — use your imagination!, Karma, a German shepherd, and Layla, a boxer. I had three: Cowboy, a yellow labrador, Callia, a rottweiler, and Little Bear, another German shepherd.

There was also an assortment of cats, so many, in fact, that I can't remember their names. Some went with Eric's ex-wife. Two — JuJu and Tiger — lived with us at Annaly. For a while, we even had a pig, but that's a long story. The list of pets in the Hutchins house during Eric's kids' childhood was legendary: ducks, birds, guinea pigs, turtles, other dogs, other cats. But by the time of the blendering, all of those pets had gone on to their reward. You can probably imagine what an important place animals held in our kids' hearts.

So what happened to the zoo crew of Annaly when we moved to Texas? Sadly, Little Bear died of bee stings on St. Croix. Our nanny kept Callia, and our housesitters kept Jake and Tiger. Karma came with us, but later relocated to a country home with a new family. Layla moved temporarily to Alabama with Marie, but rejoined us six months later. JuJu stayed with my parents until we bought the house in Houston.

And then there was Cowboy.

Cowboy was the most well-loved member of the family. Cowboy weighed in those days at 120 pounds, and not a dainty 120. He was named after the football team of the city in which he was born, but he went by several well-deserved nicknames, such as Doughboy, the Mutant, Dino Head, or simply Cowboy the Big Yellow Dog. Clark and Susanne loved him irrationally and unconditionally, and the rest of us thought he was pretty amusing, too.

Cowboy had an important job as lead watchdog at our Caribbean rainforest house. He was the alpha male, highly respected by his subordinates, who deferred to him in all things — most importantly, who got to eat what and how much out of which food bowls. He enjoyed his job and stayed in top physical condition with thrice-weekly eight-mile runs, for which he encouraged his whole platoon (us) to join him. He tried many times to do speed work by following Eric and me when we rode our bicycles from the house, but this never worked out too well (other than to ensure that in the future we always trucked the bikes to a distant starting spot). Under his watchful eye, Annaly and its inhabitants stayed safe and sound.

He also loved his time off. He took daily sojourns down to the pond in the valley to bathe. He would eagerly accompany his people on hikes up the river to the waterfalls at Caledonia, jaunts down to the tidal pools or Annaly Bay, or trips over to Sprat Hall to cavort and swim at the beach. When he had to ride in the truck, though, we had to lift him into the back. He never quite realized he could make that leap. Or maybe he actually couldn't; he was an awfully large dog.

It came time to move the dogs to Houston, and Cowboy, it turned out, was over the weight limit to fly in his kennel on the only large commercial plane leaving the island. To the horror of Clark and Susanne, we searched for a new island home for Cowboy. Our search was fruitless, though, and when it became clear that this was not going to be the solution, we put Cowboy on a diet.

Eric felt so bad about starving him that he put all six dogs on a diet, but that plan backfired, too. Cowboy ate as much as he wanted out of the other dogs' bowls before he let them have any. He lost no weight, but all the rest of the dogs got a little gaunt.

In addition to dieting and adoption, we looked into different transportation options for Cowboy. There weren't many viable alternatives, and those that we did find, such as a private plane to transport him to the mainland where he could hop a bus or train, were prohibitively expensive. Clark, Susanne, and I finally had to leave for Houston; Eric, Karma, and Cowboy stayed on the island.

When it was time for Eric to leave, too, he called to tell us that while he was going to try his best, Cowboy might not be able to come. We had a contingency plan: he could continue his guard dog function with Jake at Annaly for the housesitters while we kept looking for an adoptive family.

The day before his departure, Eric visited the airport and certain key airport and airline officials. He toted a wallet full of hundred-dollar bills, and left those he visited more well-off than he found them. Hey, remember, it's de islands, mon. People were shockingly more eager to transport Cowboy after that visit, but Eric still had to make it through the ticket agent and the baggage handlers the next day.

With his kennel, Cowboy weighed in at a whopping 135 pounds. The weight limit was 100. There was absolutely no pretending the scale was wrong, and it was unlikely that someone would conclude, "Oh, he's close enough, just send him through!" Cowboy was 35% over the weight limit. Even a casual heft of the corner of his kennel made it obvious that there was way too much dog in there.

Eric brought his wallet to the ticket counter and set some of its contents on top of the kennel when it was placed on the scale. Cowboy lost a few pounds in that transaction, Eric reclaimed his wallet, and Cowboy sailed through to baggage, "No problem, mon."

But in the baggage area, things went awry.

"No way, mon, dis dog not weigh no hunner pounds!" Eric heard the baggage handler shout. "Dis not my jawb to lift he."

In vain, Eric begged, pleaded, explained, and bribed. Not a single person was swayed by his description of his sobbing, broken-hearted children.

"Was de problem ovuh hee-yah?" another baggage handler inquired.

Eric turned at the sound of the familiar voice and looked into the face of a schoolmate from his St. Dunstan's days. Eric hailed him up, and they reminisced about old times for a few moments. Then Eric launched into the tale of woe with his old chum.

And just like that, Cowboy made it onto the plane. When Eric told us the news, Clark actually cried. (Boy, will I be in trouble for writing that.)

Eric, Cowboy, and Karma arrived well after midnight that night in Houston. Cowboy did not seem to lose any weight on the trip, nor did he display an appropriate amount of gratitude to Eric. As a new stepdad, though, Eric had forever secured his place in the hearts of Cowboy's fan club.

HOMICIDE: 22 UNNAMED VICTIMS

Blendering Principle #8: Laugh together. A lot.

AP Breaking News:

We are sad to report that twenty-two fish lost their lives in a Houston backyard pond from chlorine poisoning when a male resident of the household left water running into the pond. The bodies were discovered at about 2:00 p.m. by a traumatized resident, who first noticed something fishy when she saw a river rushing behind her bedroom's glass doors and up onto the deck. She will remain anonymous out of concern for her personal safety.

Upon investigation, she discovered a lake had formed in the backyard behind the music room. When she sought the source of the flooding, she came upon the grisly sight of twenty-two koi and goldfish belly-up in the lowest of the three ponds, with water spilling over the sides of said pond. She turned the water off and made efforts to revive the fish, but those efforts proved unsuccessful.

Among the casualties were a black "googly-eyed" fish and a two fat calico fantail goldfish. Their bodies were removed with a cat litter scoop and respectfully disposed of in a plastic Kroger bag. A brief memorial service was conducted before the fish were solemnly laid to their final rest via deposit into the dumpster.

All household residents expressed shock, horror, and grief.

"Those fish grew up in our pond. They trusted us. They were part of our family. Did you know he killed one of our cats one time, too?" said Liz Hutchins.

"Huh, what fish?" asked Clark Jackson.

"Can we go to Petco on Saturday and get some more fish? How many can we get? How much can I spend? Can I bring a friend?" queried Susanne Jackson.

"I heard he emptied a black garbage bag of frogs into the bayou. I have to question what that was all about, now," exclaimed Pamela Hutchins. "And there goes this month's water bill!"

Representatives for resident Eric Hutchins advised that he will be invoking his Fifth Amendment right to make no comment. They also wish to remind everyone that Eric was the hero that saved Cowboy.

Authorities stated that this is an ongoing investigation, but would not comment on whether the case of the dead cat has been reopened.

No charges have been filed at this time. Residents are advised to attend closely to their pets in the future, and to exercise caution when leaving them in the care of the adult male of the household.

***

The real story here was neither the fish nor the homicide. It was that in a family of such dramatic individuals, we were learning to laugh together and to keep the small stuff small. And say it with me, everyone: It's all small stuff.

FAMILY KILLING SPREE CONTINUES

Check out the email that Eric the animal killer sent to our sensitive children about our beautiful family cat, Juliet. Here's her picture in (slightly) better days:

Foreshadowing, though? Those are Eric's hands around her throat.

Here's Eric's email:

——Original Message——
From: Eric
To: Susanne
Cc: Clark; Pamela; Liz
Subject: Ju Ju
Check out this picture of Juu Juu

We all joke around about what a pain Juliet is, but we never really mean it. We all, especially Susanne, love our pets, and Eric sent this picture directly to her. This is a tragedy. I shook my head, hoping that someday they could all forgive Eric, and that Susanne would forgive me for marrying him. Or at least that they don't sock us with the bill for therapy. Or turn

out just like him. I was hoping nobody would call
Child Protective Services or the Society for Preven-
tion of Cruelty to Animals, when—

Wait a second. Something was scratching at my
office door.

Oops. False alarm! Here's JuJu, unharmed.

Still, a sick joke to pull on the kids.

But then again, that crazy sense of humor is one
of the things I love about him most. And, with
therapy, the children will recover.

SERIAL KILLER

Blendering Principle #9: Rotate the spotlight.

Y'all, I have some very disturbing news. It's been weighing heavily on my mind, but I know the right thing to do. I must speak out. I don't know about the rest of you, but it scares me to think that my neighbors could be sex offenders or serial killers. We have a home security system and a couple of big dogs, but I know that is not enough to keep a determined criminal out of our house. The house where our children live.

I know this firsthand, because there's a serial killer in our neighborhood. And she's been in our house. In fact, she's here right now — and lives upstairs.

Don't let Liz's beauty and intelligence fool you. Her (long) list of victims includes three iPods, two cameras, five phones, a desktop, and two laptops. Total body count: thirteen. She has asked for another phone for her birthday. We now struggle with the guilt of whether to knowingly send another helpless mobile to certain death. It's too late for the new laptop her grandparents just gave her; while it is healthy now, its days are surely numbered.

If you encounter her, don't be taken in by her infectious laugh. She's just trying to draw you closer, where she can zap your electronics. The perpetrator is currently under suspicion for an incident in which my iPhone was thrown to the ground, where its screen shattered and it sent a series of errant texts to Eric, calling him by (several) wrong names. She was allegedly in Florida at the time, but her story is uncorroborated.

It is clear the perpetrator gets her homicidal tendencies (and her looks) from her father, who has been linked to multiple animal deaths.

Year One: Becoming Momela

Blendering Principle #10: Expect people to exceed your expectations.

When a woman falls in mad, crazy love, I don't think her first thought is "Oh my gosh, I want nothing more in the world than for his teenage daughter to move in with us."

Mine sure wasn't.

Everything changed when Liz stepped cautiously through the door of our house in Houston and into the eager arms of Susanne and the beam of Clark's smile. Liz, AKA "The Bean," moved in her things, set up her room, and established her life here, and I became insta-stepmom to an adolescent girl. Or, as we call it at our house, the Momela.

At first we couldn't believe it. She'd left her mother and a large group of friends to live here. It was summer, so she had no one to hang out with in Houston but Clark and Susanne (and Eric and me, who, of course, are way cool).

But Liz knew her own mind. She wanted her father, siblings, family dinners, rules, sports teams, routine, and — believe it or not — chores, AKA money-making opportunities. She immersed herself in activities with an incredible will. Sure, she complained from time to time, but she eagerly pursued a busy schedule of athletic practices, swim meets, volleyball tournaments, and choir concerts; this was what she wanted. She stayed organized and made good grades without much prompting.

She wanted friends, too, and she soon had them. If there is anything more important to a girl in her early teens than her friends, I've yet to find it. We feed many extra teenagers. I am a regular at Kroger for ramen noodles, mac and cheese, microwave popcorn, diet cola, and frozen pizza. Their giggles and iTunes are our soundtrack, and the backs of their heads as they Facebook are the backdrop to our lives.

Most weekend nights we elect to run them back and forth to their (many) activities rather than going to do something ourselves. Her friends have always been nice to me and treated me with respect. By all accounts, that's a really good sign.

So why, with all that is easy and goes right, is it so difficult to be a stepparent? Being a mother itself is not always easy, but I had figured out that role. But this Momela thing. Whoa.

As lucky as I am, as good as she is, it is still sometimes hard. She can be a wee bit irrational and PMS-y. She is not always fun to be around. But the same could be said of the other kids, or even of Eric and me.

What it comes down to, most of all, is that blending parental styles and rules is hard. There is no formula to figure out what fair looks like, sounds like, and feels like for kids that have grown up under slightly different rules. We can't treat them all the same, because they are *not* all the same — but how do we reconcile that between ourselves, and with them? Will they hate each other? Will they hate us? And how do we reach the point where both Eric and I parent *all* the children, instead of divvying them up and retreating into the easiness of "You've got yours and I'll take mine"?

There were other challenges, too. Liz had been coached to hate me. I was afraid of her when she got here; afraid of the thoughts in her head, and the things she had been told. It took me awhile to realize this important truth: Children are capable of using their own minds, making their own judgments and decisions, and feeling their own feelings, far before we as parents see that they are able to.

Liz taught me this. She never once lived up to my fears, and always exceeded my expectations of how willing she was to start fresh with me and make her own decisions. She balances that with love and respect for others in her life who do not share our household's opinion of me (a goddess); this is a major feat.

When she moved in with us, Liz had to overcome a past in which she had been given almost everything material that she asked for. We couldn't have sustained that lifestyle for her if we'd wanted to, and we didn't. We welcome the chance to help our kids learn personal responsibility and to be grateful and wise.

Everyone that knew her feared Liz would hate our spendthrift ways, but she shocked us by embracing them. She has long lists of things she "needs," and we sometimes call her Liz "I Want" Hutchins, but she accepts "no" most of the time. She would prefer to eat out, but she knows how much it costs to eat at home versus at WingStop, can calculate the delta for you, and will give you a list of ten other things that money can be spent on. She knows we usually buy Kroger's store brand, and that she had better be ready to explain why a name brand is cheaper if she expects me to entertain her grocery store requests. She may not always toe the spending line, but our other kids dance around it, too.

Liz sometimes pushes me, and pushes us, mostly about being where we want her to be when we want her to be there. She would prefer a much looser interpretation of deadlines and curfews. She has a way of stalling until she gets her way by default. "I texted you to ask if I could be late," she'll say, but her text came fifteen minutes after her curfew.

But she makes amazingly good choices most of the time. There is so much pressure on teens to drink, use drugs, have sex, go to wild and unsafe parties, and do many other things that would make us shrink in horror if we knew about them. Bean asks permission for every activity and party that comes her way, but she is usually able to choose the right path with little or no prompting if we give her time to work it out for herself. We are so proud of her when she does. We hope she can keep in the front of her mind that what she says yes to now determines what we (and the world) say yes to later.

Like most teenagers, she finds it hard to enforce our rules with her friends, so I have learned to step in and help her without, I hope, embarrassing her too much. I encourage her to let me be the bad guy rather than break our rule. It's tough for a girl to say to a young (cute!) boy, "I am not allowed to have boys in this room," but she is very gracious when I say it for her.

"Liz has the strictest stepmother in the world, and I don't let boys in here, but you guys can watch a movie in either of these two other rooms," I explain.

The hardest hurdles for me to cross while becoming a true Momela have been calling Liz on behavioral issues. I hate to discipline or lecture her, and she isn't crazy about it, either. I have learned that Liz tries very, very hard to do what she is told. She is strong and will disagree if she doesn't think you are right, but she has made a visible effort to do better at things I have asked of her, like communicating her plans early and sticking to them, making eye contact with an angry adult, and saying please, thank you, and I'm sorry.

Liz is not much of a hugger with her own parents, but I hug my birth kids all the time. I still have trouble putting my arms around her and hugging her, but over time, she's become more receptive when I put my hand on her shoulder, braid her hair, or touch her face, especially when she, Eric and I are all hanging out together, watching a movie on the couch. Thank goodness for the times our kids are sick enough to need us. Once when we were all sick with the flu, I spent hours curled up in bed with Liz, Susanne and Clark. Despite the hacking coughs and violent sneezes, it was really nice.

There are shockingly few challenges, really, and Liz is a joy and easy to love. She entertains us all, and not just because we love watching her many athletic endeavors. Liz is sometimes a teenager, but she is often just a girl. We smile at her bouncing-up-and-down happiness when she announces a new boy-friend, and feel sheepishly sorry for the poor kid, knowing he'll be dumped in a week in her enthusiasm for the next one. On the way home from the theater one night, she greeted Eric with the breathless exclamation of "Oh-my-gosh-Dad-I-have-a-new-boyfriend!" He replied, "Liz, you tell me that every time I pick you up from the movies."

Time spent on appearance is endless. Her hair is curly and beautiful, the exact hair I coveted at her age. She of course hates it and straightens it until it comes out looking a lot like what God gave me on my head. She spends even more time trying on and discarding outfits (and I do mean discarding — right onto the floor, not back onto the hanger) in her daily panic over having nothing to wear.

She loves to shop, but is very careful with her own money. She will even drag me to three or four stores only to decide to buy nothing. I love this about her, that she can deprive herself and hang onto her money if she doesn't really need something or it isn't just right. And while Liz is given complete wardrobes of beautiful clothes by her mother, she usually wears the tops she chooses so carefully to spend her own money on.

I am the daytime taxi driver for the kids, and I usually have a few minutes in the car or right after Bean gets home when she will open up and talk. I think Eric treasures these moments even more than I do, because it's normally girl stuff that she doesn't ever talk to him about. Sometimes Bean practices with me on things she is scared to talk to her father or another friend or loved one about. Occasionally she even listens to my advice, and I have overheard her repeating my words verbatim to her friends as she suggests how they should handle one of the frequent scraps young girls get into.

She surprises me every now and then, this girl who is another woman's daughter. I didn't realize she was reading my writing until she said, "Pamela, you have inspired me to write, and I wrote a story. Will you read it?" I don't know if she could possibly understand how that touched my heart.

Another time, Susanne was writing words in the window fog inside the car and I asked if she wrote "I love Mommy."

"Why would I do that?" Susanne asked.

Liz, a few seconds later said, "Hey, look at my window." She had written "I love Pamela" across it. I had to stop the car to hug her and tell her she was officially now my favorite daughter. I made Susanne walk the rest of the way home[4].

---

[4] Not really.

Eric went to India for a few weeks during our first blendered year, and Liz not only was alone with Clark, Susanne, and me for a full week, but she also had three additional days of really alone time with me while Clark and Susanne visited their father. There was not a single moment where I felt she tried to take advantage of me or was anything less than fully considerate, respectful and friendly. How many stepmoms are this lucky?

I gave her plenty of rope during this time, and she handled it well. She had boys over, and she got them out of the house on time. She beat her curfew by three minutes. She went to get her nails and hair done with me. I brought her and eight friends home from a dance party, and she had her entire group out to the Suburban right on time.

But I think the biggest sign that I have become a Momela is that it has become okay for both Liz and me to be real. When she was first here, Liz was unnaturally nice, too nice, too perfect. I worried that she seemed afraid to mess up, almost like she thought we would send her away if she displeased Eric or me — especially me. I felt a little of that myself. If I had an ugly mood swing and yelled at the kids, or if Eric and I had an argument that the kids were aware of, would Liz run away? And if she did, could Eric ever forgive me?

We're over it now.

If Liz or I need to have an ugly mood swing, we have it and the world doesn't end. It's funny to look at the two of us being bad as a good sign, but it is. Occasionally we compete for her father's affection; I can feel it, but it's okay. I hope she really knows we want her here with us, no matter what. Behaving badly is not a problem anymore.

Liz Hutchins coming into my home and becoming my stepdaughter was an amazing gift. Clark and Susanne love her madly. Eric's kids are the apples of his eye, and having her here with us makes his life more complete. Liz has enriched my life, she makes me laugh, and I am proud of her.

I wasted a lot of time fretting over what I was supposed to be. Stepmother? Friend? Mentor? Annoyance? Coach? Caregiver? Taxi driver? Procurement specialist? In the first nine months she lived with us, my role slowly evolved into what it was meant to be: I am the Momela.

And, you know, this Momela thing ain't so hard after all.

THE LAST OF THE CUPCAKES

Blendering Principle #11: You never regret the extra mile.

We moved from the Caribbean to Texas, and wouldn't you know it, within one year, we had our first Texas hurricane. In the islands, wind damage was our worst fear. Here in Houston, the biggest problem is storm surge. Sure, we had a little wind damage, but boy did we have storm surge. Between the two, trees were down all over the city and our power was out for two weeks. Gas stations and grocery stores were closed. Worse, the schools were closed. We were hot, we were cranky, and we were all together.

So that is how it came to be that in the wake of Hurricane Ike, I made an accidental trip to College Station, one hundred miles away.

Yes, accidental. Don't ask.

Suffice it to say, I made the most of my visit. While I was there, I decided to stop at a lighted, air conditioned, fully stocked HEB grocery store. It was heaven, compared to the dark, sweltering, barren stores in Houston.

The sole purpose of the stop was to buy a chocolate birthday cake with chocolate icing for Liz's birthday sleepover. Without training as a pioneer or frontier woman, I didn't know how to bake a cake without power, and I didn't think it was time to experiment with foil and the gas grill. I had girls to feed sugary birthday-themed junk food to. I might not have gone to such lengths for my own kids, but when it came to my stepchildren, I felt like I had something to prove.

But, ugh. I had not reckoned on the rest of the greater Houston metroplex having the same idea at the same time. The store was jam-packed with slow-moving lines that backed up into the aisles.My first mistake was thinking I would only get a cake. My second was to go in without a cart when there were none available in the cart corral. *Well*, I thought, *if I get only a cake and a few other essentials – say milk, eggs, and bread – I will be fine.*

The layout of the HEB in College Station forced me to go through the winding, beautiful produce section before I could get to anything else. I made it through the produce section okay, but I fell prey just past it to the giant cans of whey protein powder sweetened with sucralose.

This may not sound all that exciting, but when you are determined not to consume sugar or aspartame and you are training for a Half Ironman triathlon, this is a big deal. I am usually stuck with blecky unflavored protein. But here was chocolate! And vanilla! And in the convenient-to-carry sizes of only eighty ounces each! (Roughly the size of a whiskey barrel.) I tucked one under each arm and headed to the bakery.

Don't smirk yet, it gets worse.

At the bakery, my choices were limited. Apparently all the other visiting Houstonians were having birthday sleepovers, too. I had to settle for vanilla cupcakes, but with cool icing and decorations. By this time, I was carrying the cupcakes on my head, so I headed back out through the winding, beautiful produce section to get a cart, but was stopped at the door because of my not-yet-purchased items. I stashed them on a recycling bin, then dashed out to the parking lot, where I stood and waited for a cart.

And stood. And stood.

I finally realized I needed to stalk a shopper on her way to the car and assist her by returning the cart for her. Mission accomplished, I marched my cart back into HEB and through the long, crowded, winding, and suddenly less beautiful produce section.

Clever marketers that they are, HEB puts the items everyone comes for (milk, bread, eggs) at the far the end of their carefully laid out path. Navigating through their sales-strategic aisles was like being the rat in a maze coming upon one perfect cheddar cheese after another, when all it came for was the mozzarella.

By the time I had been up and down the aisles in bumper-to-bumper traffic for half an hour, my cart was full of a month's worth of organic and gluten-free stuff I didn't need. I got one aisle further and had my *WHAT THE HELL AM I DOING* moment and went back and emptied it all out again.

Forty-five maddening minutes later, I joined the chaos around the checkout area, where I saw that my only viable choice was self checkout. I'll refrain from the profanity *that* experience deserves for the sake of my mother, who may be the only person who buys this book.

I made it to my car tired, frustrated, behind schedule, and close to tears (oh, pity Eric his mercurial wife), and I may have been just a *tiny* bit careless as I slammed down the lid of my trunk, which reeked of the gas cans I had purchased and filled earlier in the day, because you couldn't get gas cans or gas in hurricane-ravaged Houston, and we had a generator to run. A generator that was no help when it came to cupcakes, and a lot of other shit, which was why I was in College Station in the first place.

I had no one but myself to blame as the case of beautiful — albeit vanilla and not chocolate — cupcakes crashed upside-down on the dirty, September-hot pavement. The top popped open on impact.

I brushed the gravel sprinkles off two dozen smushed cupcakes that now looked like they'd had a visit from Hurricane Ike. I stuffed them back into their holder. I was not going back into the HEB, not even to prove something to one of my stepkids.

The misshapen cupcakes and I made it home by about 6:00 p.m., and they were consumed enthusiastically and with good humor by my really wonderful stepdaughter and her friends and siblings.

The next week, one sad, mushed-up cupcake re-mained in the box as a reminder of the melee. I didn't have the heart to throw it out yet.

THE 3/5 RULE

Blendering Principle #12: Row in the same direction.

When it comes to the stability and behavior of our five kids, we have a 3/5 rule: At any given time, three of them will implode and two will temporarily impersonate angels. On rare occasions, we'll luck out and enjoy a short 2/5 period. Less rare but still infrequently, we suffer through a 4/5. We've never had to endure a 5/5. We once had twelve hours of a 0/5, and it was the most peaceful twelve hours of our life together.

What does a 4/5 look like?

Ugly.

Let's take a peek at an old blog entry from my *Road to Joy* website:

It's a 4/5 day. Eric flew to Tampa at the request of his oldest for some emergency car shopping (don't ask), leaving me solo with two of the three remaining miscreants. A side effect of 4/5 days is that the rosy outlooks of the parents crumble under the onslaught of kid issues. That day was no exception. So if you count Eric and me falling apart, we were really have a 6/7 day. *Holy crapoly*

The day started out super fine for me (and it is all about me). I made a friend IRL. My new laptop rocked. I finished the *Annalise* rewrites. I landed a big new project, which meant $$$, but I only had to manage the work, not perform it. My favorite kind!

I knew I was on shaky turf, though, because of the implosion of Thomas followed by Liz's emotional meltdown coupled with the standoff with Marie, then of course Clark had to come home with a backpack full of zeroes and mouth full of lies, so, yep, there we were at midnight, all of us frayed and frazzled, and I was annoyingly right, as always.

And absolutely worn to a nub.

For those of you that have secretly hated me for having a nearly perfect life, I have tried to tell

you that appearances can be deceiving, but nobody ever listens to me. Trust me, if I wrote
anonymously, the stories I would tell about our
family would have you gloating and chortling.

"Their kids are way worse than ours!"

"She never gets out of her pajamas, even to
shower!"

"Her husband is wicked sarcastic!"

"They really do want to kill Clark!"

"Woo hoo!"

Yep, it can suck. The shit can really hit the blender, ya know? But when it's good, man oh man, it's the
best. So we have learned to handle it as partners.
Usually as partners. Ideally as partners. Seriously, we
at least partner on how we are going to handle it.
Partnering on parenting is a tenet of our ROA, after
all. It's there for a reason. It's a goal we strive for but
can't always attain.

Early on, we made a pact to handle all parenting
together, but to do so with consistent rules across
households. Eric consulted his ex, who told him she
had no intentions of enforcing his rules and didn't
particularly care what they were. She would do it her
way and he would do it his way.

Okay, that didn't go so well. Nor did it ever improve. So we worked around it, as partners.

In the summer of Year One, we sat together in front of the recalcitrant and sobbing Liz as Eric explained why we didn't want to see "Clark is such an asshole" statuses on Facebook anymore. Even when he was.

We stood side by side as I talked (again) to Clark about the consequences of lying.

We sat around the kitchen table with Susanne as we laid out her penance for not informing us of her whereabouts.

Not all situations lend themselves to a partnership. Some of our biggest blowouts as a couple are over the times one of us wings it alone on the parenting. After a few of those debacles, we decided that partnering can also mean communicating after the fact, even if a side-by-side or a pre-chat on the issues is preferable. Partnering means no secrets, even if it means one-on-one instead of two-on-one discussions.

Sometimes the kids' issues are about one of us, because we are a lot like a real family, where the kids get mad at the Momela or Dad or other relevant household authority figures. We back each other. We help each other apologize when Eric is wrong. Okay, and when I'm wrong, too.

We have faced some tough, tough moments. For a full year, two of the five kids refused to interact with us in opposition to choices one or the other or both of us made vis à vis them. At any point during those long months, we could have chosen to cave in. But instead of caving, we partnered. We cried. We held each other. We re-discussed the issues. What values could we absolutely not compromise on enforcing? What price was too high? Which behaviors could we tolerate and which ones could we not? We wondered if the long standoffs would ever end. We anguished over love and time lost. We stood together as we stood our ground. And we celebrated together when it ended.

Years later, I can share the formula that worked for our parenting partnership most of the time, and I can promise it won't work all the time or for everyone. But I hope it helps.

Communicate Before, Communicate During, Communicate After[5]

1. Decide upfront on your absolutes

---

[5] My apologies — this structure comes from my work life. I just can't help it.

2. No secrets

3. Stall with your child until you can discuss with your partner

4. Together is better

5. Don't be stingy with *I'm sorry* and *I love you*

6. We are here to raise responsible humans, not to make friends

But even when we followed our own principles to the tee, the 3/5 rule still came into play.

That damn rule. It gets us every time.

SHOTGUN WEDDING

Blendering Principle #13: Celebrate together, every chance you get.

Two eager children forced Eric and me to renew our wedding vows. Not quite a shotgun wedding, but almost. It all started when Susanne was using my laptop and clicked the wrong subfolder, ending up at a slide show of pictures of Eric and me. No, not *that* kind of slide show; it was of our wedding pictures. Clark started watching, too.

We hadn't had anyone but the two of us at our beach wedding on St. John, and we'd caught a lot of grief for that from the kids over the years. Clark and Susanne decided to do something about it.

Clark got online and looked up wedding ceremonies. Susanne ran outside and found a few scraggly blossoms on our hydrangea and made a prickly bouquet. Clark retrieved my dress from our storage closet; someone played dress-up before I got home. It was scary how well my dress fit eleven-year-old Susanne.

Now all they needed was us.

Eric got home from work at 6:25 and the kids accosted him immediately. We had plans to go out for barbecue at 6:30 sharp, so they were on a mission to deliver us (again) into wedded bliss, chop chop. I'd arrived earlier than Eric, and Susanne had already dressed me for the surprise occasion. Clark and Susanne pushed me in front of Eric, and the ceremony began.

Clark officiated, in a very Clark-like manner: over-the-top. He insisted on calling Eric "Eric Ralph Hutchins the second," despite Eric's explanation that there was no ERH the first. The vows were very, very long and involved such requirements as "Pamela to love Eric and his favorite team the Arizona Cardinals," and "Eric to always provide Pamela with a house to live in." We finally had to cut him off, or I'm sure he'd still be going.

Susanne played "Here Comes the Bride" continuously on her flute throughout the entire five minutes.

Liz, sixteen, was on a date so she missed all the festivities, and I am sure it broke her heart, although she forgot to tell us if it did.

The only miss was that due to the abrupt end to the ceremony ("I now pronounce you Mr. and Mrs. Eric Ralph Hutchins the Second. You may now kiss Pamela Kay Fagan Hutchins"), Susanne forgot to take pictures.

We celebrated our nuptials by watching *Kung Fu Panda* together later that night and going for a twelve-mile run the next morning. (Only us on the run, not Clark and Susanne.) Now they can't complain that they missed out on the party anymore.

THIS STEPMOM THING TAKES RESOLVE.

Blendering Principle #14: Lead by (good) example.

Getting married on January first means I always get sappy over New Year's. So after a year or three, I realized I could do something with all that emotional energy. Something productive. Something that looked delightfully like a plan for the year. Ah, resolutions.

And I'm sharing them, because I'm awesome that way. Maybe they'll work for you, too.

They went something like this:

1. <u>I want to make my husband feel ten feet tall this year.</u>

I can't believe I have been blessed to be with The One and feel this mad, crazy love in my forties, and be lucky enough at the same time that he is a kind, generous, hard-working, romantic, fun, ethical person. Given that we believe we were destined to be together, it would have sucked if he was a drug dealer, or gambling addict, or wife beater. I won the lottery. Every day, I need to make sure he realizes it, because he deserves to feel amazing about himself.

2. I will be a role model to our children, demonstrating hard work, good judgment, well-roundedness, joy, love, kindness, and responsibility.

When I fall short, I will show contrition. I will love them, and make sure their development is as high a priority to me as I want it to be to them. I will stay engaged and help them be responsible and make good choices. I will support their endeavors, encourage their efforts, and provide the structure and discipline that we humans need to thrive. I will enjoy them and be proud of them. I will try really, really, really hard not to expect more of them than I do of myself.

The clock hand spins crazy fast with our children, with two already out of the house and rarely in our lives, and three racing toward their own appointment with adulthood. Already, one of the last three is rarely with us for the free times, and mostly only here for the routines. Without sacrificing fiscal responsibility, I will make a concerted effort to create joy and memories as a family.

3. <u>This year, I won't engage with anyone or anything that brings hate into my life.</u>

It is really hard to keep hating some people, and really easy to remember why you have hated others. Either way, it requires a lot of energy that I don't want to give away to negativity. I'm saving my energy to bring positive light into the lives of myself and my loved ones.

4. <u>This year I will finish and publish two books, even if I have to publish them myself.</u>

And I will be proud of them, no matter what anyone else thinks, because they were very hard to do, and because just the completion of them represents the fulfillment of my dreams and goals.

5. <u>I will keep up my financial contribution to our household, both in terms of income and in terms of fiscal responsibility.</u>

I will not let us grow fat, lazy, indulgent, or complacent, especially in these scary economic times.

We have hit "cash" break-even . . . barely . . . and possibly only temporarily . . . for the first time in three years, while still racking up debt for someday. We have to continue replacing the sandy foundation with bedrock.

6. <u>I will be the best athlete I have ever been</u>, overcoming the genes my father described as "piss-poor protoplasm, poorly put together" that have always mired me in lower mediocrity.

Through effort and consistency, will and endurance, I will reach for new distances, new events, and make my best times. I will not let people who make fun of me, or are snide or derisive about my modest ability, deter me from being the best I can be and doing more than anyone sitting on the sofa.

7. <u>This year I will play the piano and sing with my whole heart</u>.

I will set my carefully tucked away library of poems, that I always knew were songs, to the music I hear in my head each night as I fall asleep. I will play them no matter how bad they are. I will make my cat very happy as she sits beside me while I play and curls herself around my teacher's ankles when he sits down at the piano with us.

8. <u>I will do things to let our relatives know how important and beloved they are to us</u>.
Our kids and our relationship will be our top priorities, but I will do as much as I can to reach out to the people that shape who we are, and enjoy and appreciate them.

9. <u>I will work with my husband to increase the presence of spirituality, thankfulness, and love of God in our home</u>.
We have so, so, so much to be thankful for. We all face hardships, but they don't define us. If we look back at them, they can defeat us and cause us to lose sight of the gifts we are given. We will face forward, toward the future, toward positivity, toward our blessings, and we will be grateful.

10. <u>I will not let this list overwhelm me, and I will forgive myself when I do not live up to it</u>.
I will take a deep breath, put my eyes back on the summit, and take another step. Mount Everest is a tall mountain, but you climb it only one step at a time.

LEAVING ANNALY

Blendering Principle #15: Someone always moves your cheese. Get over it.

Not so long ago and not so willingly, my family and I left my dream house in the islands for Houston. When we told people, "We're moving from St. Croix to Houston," they reacted like we'd contracted a terminal illness. There's something about that city that seems like the end of the line. And bless its heart, Houston is neither beautiful nor comfortable. If the heat and humidity don't kill you, the traffic might. People don't dream of vacationing in Houston. Hell, I can't even get my parents to visit me.

It was painful to emigrate from the U.S. Virgin Islands, the ultimate fantasy destination. And we didn't just live in the Virgin Islands. We lived in Annaly, tucked into the rainforest on the island of St. Croix. The best way I know to conjure up the wonderfulness of this place is to give you an excerpt from my novel, *Leaving Annalise*. In this semi-autobiographical scene, Katie, the protagonist, sees Annalise/Annaly for the first time while on a guided hike through the rainforest.

***

We had hiked for nearly two hours when Rashidi gave us a hydration break and announced that we were nearing the turnaround point, and that it would be a special treat: a modern ruin. He explained that a bad man, a thief and a thug, had built a beautiful mansion in paradise, named her Annalise, and then been taken away for drug trafficking by the federal authorities, leaving her forsaken and half-complete. No one had ever finished her, and the rainforest had moved fast to claim her. Wild horses roamed her halls, colonies of bats filled her eaves, and who knows what lived below her, in the depths of her cisterns. We would eat our lunch there, then turn back for the—much easier, he promised—hike down.

When the forest parted to reveal Annalise, we all drew in a breath. She was amazing: tall, austere, and a bit frightening. The tension grew in our group. What woman doesn't love going to an open house? And here we were visiting a mysterious mansion with a romantic history in a tropical rainforest.

Graceful, flamboyant trees and grand pillars marked the entrance to her gateless drive. On each side of the overgrown road were tropical fruit trees of every description, and the fragrance was pungent, the air drunk with fermenting mangos and ripening guava, subtly undercut by the aroma of bay leaves. It was a surreal orchard, its orphaned fruit unpicked, the air heavy and still, bees and insects the only thing stirring besides our band of turistas. Overhead the trees' branches met in the middle of the road and were covered in vines with trailing pink flowers. The sun shone through the dim light occasionally in narrow beams.

We climbed up Annalise's ten uneven front steps and stepped through what would have been an imposing double front door into a great room with thirty-five-foot ceilings. The oohs and aahs began. We gazed up in wonder at her intricate tongue-in-groove cypress ceiling with mahogany beams, her improbable stone fireplace.

We explored her three stories, room after room unfolding as we discussed what each was to have been. Balcony floors with no railings jutted from two sides of the house. A giant concrete pool hovered partway out of the ground. How could someone put in so much work, build something magnificent, create such hope, and leave her to rot?

Gradually, a few ughs replaced the oohs as we discovered that we had to step over horse manure and bat guano in every room. Dead gungalos by the thousands crunched under our feet. One woman put her hand on a wall and ended up with dung between her fingers and gunked into her ostentatious diamond ring, which for some inexplicable reason she'd worn on a rainforest hike. Annalise was not for the faint of heart, and I suppressed my urge to run for a broom. What she could have been was so clear; what she might still be was staggering.

***

So how could my husband and I just pack up the kids and move to the continental forty-eight, leaving the magic, the magnificence of Annaly behind?

Well, for starters, the prayer we prayed — never to leave Annaly, to live our lives in the islands — was answered with a "No," and a "Houston."

Houston? Houston? Oh why, God, Houston?

God answered. Jobs. Opportunities for the kids. Grownup stuff, the kinds of things offered by a city that stands sturdy in the face of economic storm all around it.

Oh yeah, that stuff.

The islands were beautiful. But they were a lot like Annaly: plenty of ugh to go with the oooohs. Yucky grocery stores, substandard health care, government corruption, and no Target around the corner.

So we moved to Houston with the whole family in outright rebellion. The kids assured us we were ruining their lives and that someday they would return to their true island home. Annaly summoned up all the powers of heaven and earth to keep us there and threw crisis after crisis in our path: burglaries, storms, sales fallen through, money pouring through our fingers. But we had no choice. We had committed. We moved to Houston.

And here's the part that came as a shock to us, the part that everyone believes I am making up: We loved it.

Houston, possibly because of our (extraordinarily) low expectations, was wonderful. Our fears of traffic, bad public schools, horrible weather, a soulless metroplex, and a bastion of unbridled social conservatism and neo-fascism? All for naught. Who would have ever guessed Houston would elect a lesbian Democrat as mayor? If that doesn't blow all the stereotypes, I don't know what will! We carefully planned a life here to take advantage of the best the city had to offer and to avoid the rest, and discovered that Houston rocks for the Hutchins-Jacksons clan.

Ah, a lesson. We learn. We adapt. We move on. If we are lucky and have the right attitude, we thrive. I am thankful for my time in the islands. I will never forget the people and the gorgeous turquoise and green eighty-degree trade-wind-kissed memories. Annaly will be the standard by which all my future homes are judged, and it is a high, high standard. But as I sit here in my much smaller house in central Houston with nary a flamboyant tree in sight, I have to smile.

T'ings are exactly how dere s'posed to be, mon. T'ings dem is alright. Irie.

I'M PRETTY SURE THIS IS INAPPROPRIATE.

Clark and I saw these by the cash register at our local Blockbuster. I asked the cashier what he thought about Hot Mama and he said, "I think I'd stick a peppermint in and eat it like a lollipop."

I am not kidding. You can ask my (damaged) son.

I am pretty sure this is inappropriate, and I'm a
certified expert in what is inappropriate, at least

according to the state court in Bexar County, Texas. It's a long story; just trust me on it.

Way to go, Blockbuster!

To those of you worried that these risqué snacks might pickle Clark's brain, I must admit that I might have done that already myself. When Clark and Susanne were only eleven and nine, I took them to see *Talladega Nights* in the theater. It cracked me up, but I spent most of the movie blushing with my hands over my own eyes and ears. I wish there had been someone to do the same for my kids, but the only other person there was my mother, whose hands were over her own eyes.

I'd feel guilty about this, except . . . come to think of it . . . you can rent *Talladega Nights* at **Blockbuster**. Maybe I can blame it on Blockbuster.

Recently, I rented *Youth in Revolt* and allowed my teenagers to watch it unsupervised. When I watched it later, I was horrified to discover that most of the movie glorified teenage sex and criminal behavior. I know — Mother of the Year! It occurred to me that I'd probably need therapy to deal with the thought of my kids watching it — but really, I wanted to complain to Blockbuster.

Then I cleaned Clark's room.

I do not make it a habit to clean Clark's room, or even to go into it, if I can help it. In fact, I don't go upstairs to the "dormitory" where our three youngest kids live any more than absolutely necessary. My slightly-OCD brain short-circuits when I can't see the bedroom floor, and when I stripped the sheets off Clark's bed and discovered a *Sports Illustrated Swimsuit Edition* stashed between his mattress and box springs. I studied the cover carefully to figure out where my child could have gotten such contraband.

You can imagine my dread when I discovered the common link. I don't know who this Eric Hutchins is, but I am calling Blockbuster to complain about him IMMEDIATELY.

TEXTATION

I love that my kids — step and birth — carry cell phones. When I want to know how or where they are, they are never more than a text away, with a picture to prove it if my husband and I have doubts. When they need me, vice versa. But the technology of texting has made one thing more difficult in our home: stepparenting.

When a child wants to criticize one of us, a birth parent is never more than a text away. When a birth parent is angry at one of us, a child is never more than a text away. It's a new twist on an old phenomenon: badmouthing the ex and his or her current life.

It's like having an angry, slightly drunk forty-four-year-old man sitting down with us for meals. Or a forty-eight-year-old woman and her mom or boyfriend riding in our car with us and attending family outings. Yet when we look up, all we see is one of our kids sitting across the table. A kid that goes from happy and interactive to withdrawn and borderline rude in the flash of a red light and a toneless vibration.

This phenomenon works in the reverse as well. I don't ignore the impact on our exes that our missives may have. It's a conundrum. We want to encourage our kids to have open and frequent communication with all of their parents, including us when they are with the other parent, and at the same time, it would be super nice to have an occasional break from the hating.

The kids shouldn't have to be the gatekeepers. They are already under enough pressure. Their relationships with both of their birth parents are sacred. So rational discussion with them about whether a stream of texts criticizing the stepparents or custodial birth parents is in the best interests of the child? Tricky to impossible.

Some rules are easy. We established no-cell-phone zones at the table and during small group gatherings or conversations. We talked to each of them about setting their own limits, within reason, and not letting any of us as parents cross them. "Life won't end if you step away from the phone," we tell them. We try to demonstrate the behavior we want from them and encourage them to expect it of others, including their other parents.

Truly, though, it leaves me stymied. The situation started festering on day one. It makes me long for the good old days of high-priced long-distance phone calls and "Oh Dad, don't make me" handwritten letters with envelopes and stamps.

At one point, Eric and I finally accepted defeat and decided that all would work itself out when the children were old enough to understand the difference between passion and poison, between guidance and manipulation. We decided to focus on positive parenting, on instilling accountability and self-sufficiency in respectful, empathetic young people. And pray that we are not the poisonous, manipulative texters.

Blendering Principle #16: Everything in its own time and place.

A FAMILY THAT SWEATS TOGETHER GETS TOGETHER.

Blendering Principle #17: Make health and well-being a visible priority.

No discussion of our family culture is complete without recognizing the importance that sports — especially bicycling, swimming, and triathlons — play in our blendering. Well, that and watching football, but I'll cover that later.

My husband is an engineer, but for years he has competed in triathlons, and for many of those years he co-owned a triathlon/bicycle store. When Eric and I first married, Susanne told her teacher that her new stepfather was a bicycle mechanic. Which he was, just not professionally.

We have bicycle tools and stands everywhere. Seven bicycles hang from hooks in our playroom ceiling, and our large and unattractive bicycle trainers have a permanent place of honor in our formal living room with the best view of the TV and position relative to the speakers. It's easy to see how Susanne could make that mistake.

None of the kids quite share our enthusiasm for bicycling, but the bicycles come with us everywhere: mountain biking at the lake, road bicycling at Brazos Bend, or simply riding the bikes to the pool. That's what we do as a family for Mother's Day and Father's Day.

We have done multiple family races, but only short ones so far. However, we have semi-firm commitments from four of the kids to do the MS 150 bicycling event from Houston to Austin at some point. All three of our daughters swim competitively, and two of our girls and counting have their eyes on the Half Ironman prize, with a possible Ironman someday. Four of the kids came and cheered us on for our first Half Iron. We look forward to doing the same for them. It's our thang. It's their thang. It's who we are.

WE AIN'T NO JACKSON FIVE, BUT WE TRY.

That's the love of my life, on the right.

Blendering Principle #18: Help me help you.

My husband Eric and I like to get it on, in music and athletics. And when we do those right, in a lot of other ways, too. Yeah, baby! You've probably already figured out that we're one of those couples who make you want to puke. As part of our ROA, we made specific commitments to each other. Remember this part?

> *Our relationship's purpose is to create a loving, nurturing, safe environment which*
> - *makes a positive, joyful difference in each other's lives,*
> - *encourages spiritual, emotional and physical needs and development*

Sounds good, doesn't it? But what does it really mean when it comes to our day-to-day lives?Well, hang on, cowboys and cowgirls, 'cause I'm a'gonna tell ya.

In the second year of our marriage, I took piano lessons, a birthday gift from my parents. I didn't ask for the lessons. My parents gave them to me because my husband was trying to get me to drag my rusty fingers back to the keyboard and, with help from a little steel wool and Rustoleum, play again. For the life of me, I couldn't figure out why.

In his pre-Pamela life, Eric had immersed himself in his passions for triathlon and music (slappin' da bass). When we first got together, I didn't understand that they were an escape for him. I thought my job was to enable him to continue to pursue them. He showed me a video of his band opening for 10,000 Maniacs, and I said, "Cool! Join another band."

Wrong answer, Pamela. He wanted to do it together. Music, that is.

After two years of marriage in which he refused to do his beloved sport, I finally got it about endurance triathlon. I aspired to marathons, and I had done sprint triathlons. Endurance triathlon intimidated me. But unless I participated with him in endurance triathlon, he would never do it again.

What was it our ROA said? Ah, yes: *Encourages spiritual, emotional and physical needs and development.* Duh, me. I got it. He wanted me to do a Half Ironman.

So I jumped in with both feet, and we did a Half Ironman five months later. Somewhere along the way, endurance sports became important to me as an individual, too. Although, undoubtedly, I sucked, and still do.

Even after I figured out that I needed to be a tri-athlete for Eric to continue in triathlon, it didn't register that I needed to be a musician for Eric to continue in music. I'm told I'm pretty slow for a smart woman.

I had begged, pleaded, cajoled, and praised his playing. We attended a rockin' reunion with his hilarious high school garage band. We went to see his former bandmates play in their new bands. He was invited to practice and play onstage with many groups. I bought him a new strap with a big smiling sunshine on it, and I talked him through his old playlists. But he just would not open the Fender case and get out his darn bass.

I procrastinated for nine months after receiving the gift certificate for the piano lessons, and I had only three more months before it expired. Eric quit making his gentle inquiries and just let me stew in it. I told myself I didn't have time. I thought of all the things I could do that were less self-indulgent: work, housework, errands, writing, training.

But, again, what did that pesky ROA say? Here it is: *Makes a positive, joyful difference in each other's lives.*

Darn it. Woman up, Pamela.

I booked the first lesson. And Eric glowed.

"I heard a song that we could play together, with Clark on drums, Susanne on flute, you on keyboard, and Liz singing with you," he said before I had even had my first lesson.

He explained his concept of bringing together each of the kids' interests in music into family jam sessions. It dawned on me — finally — that he wanted a family experience. I was not self-indulgent for booking the lessons. Rather, I was selfish in not booking them, because I'd prevented it from happening for everyone else.

After my first lesson, I sheepishly told him that I had to practice scales that night to strengthen my fingers.

"I'll play them with you," he said.

Eric had not brought his bass out in six months. But sure enough, for an hour we played scales together, with him riffing a little every now and then. It was a magical time.

He told the kids about his family jam idea. The excitement level in the house shot up, and they hung out with us while we went through the repetitive and not-very-exciting exercise of putting our fingers to work. The next night at dinner Clark offered to get online and hunt for songs for us to play. Susanne suggested we record a Christmas song on a CD to send with our Christmas cards. Liz sang through the entire dinner, got her choir music, and asked me to accompany her on the piano. The whole atmosphere changed, in a very good way.

We ended up recording a wonderfully awful version of "Deck the Halls." You can still see the craptastic end-product under Videos on my personal Facebook page. Don't believe me? Check it out. I've left it open for public viewing and ridicule.

Every day I get a little smarter about how to be Eric's wife in our blendered family. I enjoy the smile I see on his face now when I say something like "I think we should add Golden Earring's 'Twilight Zone' to our playlist, honey." And even more when we do.

After we get back from bicycling, of course.

WHAT'S FOR DINNER?

Blendering Principle #19: Flexibility is the key to air power.

With three teenagers and two working parents in our house, our meals gradually sank to the lowest common food denominator.

"What's for dinner?" asks a teenager.

"[Insert any non-junk-food answer here]," says the parent.

"Ah man, can I just make some [pizza, macaroni and cheese, chocolate chip waffles, etc.]?" the teenager replies.

We tried to cook healthy at the beginning of our blender days. Really, we did. It was hard, though. For starters, our eating backgrounds were quite different. One household ate out a lot and didn't believe in leftovers. You'd think I'd put a plate of live hantavirus in front of Liz and Eric when I served leftovers. The foods we liked were different, too. Liz and Eric thought my cool pineapple boats were dessert. Clark and Susanne didn't get spaetzle and veggies with chicken legs, bone-in.

When only two of the five of us (Momela and Eric/Dad) ate the good-for-you stuff, we quit making it. But that didn't solve our problems. Kids need nutrition for their brains and bodies, and all of us participate in athletics. That means more, not less, in terms of nutritional needs. We gave them snazzy pill holders to encourage vitamins, but even when the kids take them — and they rarely do without two live witnesses and a cattle prod — that's not the same as eating the right food.

Eric and I suffer if we eat badly. Every mile of triathlon training we put on our bodies hurts worse if we do not eat well. Eric has high cholesterol and blood pressure. Migraines plague us both. Gluten and sugar make my stomach and body hurt, and I am a devotee of Dr. Hotze[6] and bioidentical hormones.

So, we picked up a copy of *Cooking Light: The Essential Dinner Tonight Cookbook*. The cookbook contained 350 healthy meals that looked fun and yummy, so we figured it was worth a try. And no, this is not an ad for *Cooking Light*. It just worked so well that I decided to be specific in sharing exactly the culinary Bible we turned to.

It's easy to use. The instructions are clear enough even for my ADHD son to follow, as they tell you exactly what to do on each dish and in what order. "While the pasta boils, prepare the sauce. As the sauce simmers, cook the . . . "

------

[6] www.hotzehwc.com

Of course, we reverted to type and instituted a plan. Each family member picks a menu at the beginning of the week. With five of us, that means two free nights are left open for junk. (Having junk nights is critical to our success with the kids.) We made a rule that everyone must honor the selections of other family members.

Our first few trips to the grocery store entailed buying things we hadn't stocked in the past. As a result, I'm in love with spicy black sesame oil and rice vinegar now. We have to double each recipe; they feed four normal people, but that only equals three in our household. Bonus: there are enough leftovers to feed the parents lunch the next day.

We've stuck with the plan for a year and counting, and noticeably absent is any kvetching about food. The excitement level about picking and trying something new remains high, even for the child that previously ate only chicken, french fries, and waffles.

Certainly, we plan in advance more than before, and we combine careful grocery shopping with scheduled meal prep time. Our parent and child workout schedules often conflict and are quite heavy, so that is a challenge, but none of the meals take longer than forty-five minutes to prepare. And of course we improvise a bit to meet our health needs.

Now when we get the text asking "What's for dinner?" it's followed by "Whose night is it to pick? Are we having the one I picked?"

I savor those moments.

Unfriending

Blendering Principle #20: Facebook is FOREVER.

The technological and social ramifications of divorce and blendering can be overwhelming for both kids and parents. Texting is just the beginning; social media introduces a whole new world of confusion and challenges. Facebook, Twitter, and blogs dominate many of our kids' free hours, even if you aren't conscious of it. What kind of conduct are they witnessing in your news stream? Facebook is a public forum. Don't let any promises of privacy lead you away from this truth. Assume that everyone, including your kids, can see what you put up there, and act accordingly. No nasty "I hate my ex" statuses or snide comments on your girlfriend's wall that will drag the kids into your drama, mama.

And how should you deal with your ex on Facebook? Sure, you can change your relationship status and unfriend him or her. But what about all the friends who are his IRL friends and relatives? Yes, your ex is going to be friends with the kids, and thus the ex and his entourage will see any family photos and news you post that tags your kids.

Is it okay for your ex to friend your IRL friends and family? What is and is not OK? The answer often comes down to the status of the real-life relationship between exes, their motivation for wanting to remain connected to each other's worlds, and the potential impact on their kids. The best interests of the children trump all.

Here's my attempt at some basic rules, for which I welcome dissent, because the social norms in this area are not solid yet:

1. If you can, talk to your ex and agree on your own norms. Yeah, yeah, I know, you hate each other and can't talk about anything. But you need to get the heck over that, and fast. This is the least of your issues.

2. Relationship not good enough to talk it out? Well then, that's the answer. Your relationship is bad, so stay out of each other's worlds. You can gently disengage on Facebook and leave your

former friends none the wiser. If you feel the need to explain it to your ex-mother-in-law, then do so. It's not about her, and it will help keep peace in her world. She may even appreciate that.

3. If in doubt, don't. Ask yourself how much of your ex you want to see in your News Feed, and you'll probably have the answer to how much of you they want to see in theirs. So don't friend their IRL circle of loved ones unless you've worked it out in #1 above and you're sure it's OK.

4. No matter what the answers are to #1-3, ask yourself WHY. Why am I friending this person? Is it in any part to drive my ex insane, to spy on him, to manipulate the children, to one-up them in the game of "look who's in my corner?" If so, be a grownup. Don't do it.

5. If you share kids, multiply all of the above by a factor of ten in favor of best interests of the children.

It infuriated me when my ex friended my family and friends on Facebook. It made me even angrier that they accepted. However, I can't expect my Southern mother to have the discourtesy to turn down a friend request. That's like turning down a social invitation to dinner in her world. It just isn't *done*.

I can and did ask my ex to unfriend her. We talked about it. I told him I felt spied on, that I thought it sent a confusing message to our kids, that it was disruptive emotionally to our blended family, and that I felt he was trying to come between my family and friends and their relationship with my new spouse. And, by talking, guess what happened?

We reached an agreement.

He didn't want me in his world. So he would gently begin the process of disengagement from mine, and move on to one of his own. It didn't happen overnight. He still pops up in my News Feed occasionally, commenting on someone or other's status. But much less than before, which makes us both happier, which in turn makes it easier on our children.

We wanted away from each other. That's why we divorced. Social media made it harder. But imagine his special pain about the fact that I'm a writer. With a website and blog. And published books that talk about him. If for no other reason than his patience

with all of this, I can forgive him for a heck of a lot of
other sins.

I AM THE SWAMI.

Did I mention sports is our thang, a key facet of our blendered culture? Well, it is. It is and then some. So, since my husband and I strive to instill the best of virtues in our precious offspring, we leapfrogged from sports to culture to a family football betting pool. Sports + betting = virtue. Right?

That's the version of the story my husband swears by, anyway. When he first talked me into these shenanigans, it went something like this:

Eric: I have a really cool game called Swami that I think we can bond over with the kids. It's a football betting game.

Me: Football and betting? Are we corrupting them? Is this a CPS-intervention type of thing?

Eric: No, nothing like that. We're not betting money, anyway, just bragging rights. It's a learning opportunity. It's not even just the probabilities, statistics, mathematics, athletics, and football. It's pride and social consciousness, it's perseverance and the human psyche. It's structure and rules. It's doing something with the kids besides arguing about chores and homework.

Me: Slow down, Knute Rockne. It's betting. On football. {Eye roll}

I relented, of course, and our family Swami game was born.

Eric had created Swami many, many years ago as an engineering group leader. He was looking for ways to encourage unintimidating traffic into his office so he could keep an open dialogue with his employees. The young engineers were in and out of his office several times a day to look at the big Swami whiteboard on his wall — mission accomplished. And it was fun. Now, we could debate whether he could have picked a more gender-neutral game, but as an avid football fan, you won't hear me speak against his choice.

Blendering Principle #21: The best time to talk is when you don't have anything particularly important to talk about.

Each year the engineers added layers of complex rules to the game, as engineers love to do. They considered every possible outcome and planned for every possible issue. They deemed their rules the Swami Constitution, a copy of which I have saved to my hard drive, should any of you suffer from insomnia and wish to peruse a copy. I dare you to ask for it.[7]

What is this Swami game of which I speak, you ask? Here's the rundown: Each week of the football season, last year's Swami winner selects four college and four pro games for the players to predict the scores on. Whoever guesses the right outcome the most times comes in first for the week, earning 1

---

[7] pamela@pamelahutchins.com

point, with 2 points to 2nd place, 3 points to 3rd place, 4 points to 4th, and so forth. If there is a tie, the winner is determined based on the total of the point spreads between their picks and actual scores. Over the season, each week's score is cumulated for each player, and the person with the lowest cumulative points at the end of the season wins.

Simple enough, right? Ha.

The real key to the game is strategy, fair or foul. For instance, the Swami Constitution requires the players to designate a fave pro and college team. There are loyalty penalties for picking wrongly against one's favorite teams, so a smart Swami will deliberately choose games that test the players' loyalties. If one of the week's games includes the Cowboys, who are Clark's favorite pro team, and Clark picks the Cowboys to lose but they actually win, he gets a loyalty penalty point. Yet if the Cowboys suck (which they usually do), and Clark picks them to win because he doesn't want to risk a loyalty penalty point, the Swami can safely assume Clark will have picked this game wrong. Thus, it is a huge advantage to be the Swami and get to pick the games.

Another favorite tactic? Some players post their picks, then change them minutes before the deadline to try to psych other players into following fake or bad picks. You aren't supposed to copy other players' picks . . . but the power of suggestion is a dangerous thing. Especially if your name is Susanne.

The most popular element of the game is smack talking. Our family has this down to an art form. Clark has learned to lure Eric into side bets on Cowboys/Aggies v. Cardinals/Lobos statistics by a slow build of trash talking about Eric's teams. He waits until he is sure he has goaded Eric into the appropriate level of emotionally frenzied vulnerability, then suggests Eric put his money where his mouth is. Alas, Eric falls for it every time. Clark bought an iTouch with his winnings from Eric one year.

Related to the smack-talking element is the naming convention. Each player must have a name. In their first season, they can pick their own name, but often the names are "strongly suggested," as in the case of Eric's boss, who accepted the handle of "Darth" in honor of Darth Vader, a nickname given to him by his ex-wife that his employees found highly amusing.

At the end of the season, if the Swami loses, the players pick a new name for him. Eric was Swami one year, but lost the position to me for the next; I named him Captain Underpants (you don't want to know). The winner of the season becomes the new Swami for the next year, and the person in last place is named after the worst coach[8] of the year in pro-football. In 2010, honors went to Coach Fox and Clark.

In years past, Eric limited his Swami contests to work, but in 2007, he doubled up and had Swami-at-work and Swami-at-home. He felt certain he would obliterate the competition at home, but he failed to take into account how emotionally attached he is to the Arizona Cardinals and University of New Mexico Lobos, and his score suffered heavily because of it.

He also underestimated how badly his most beloved ones wanted him to lose. Strategy at our house in Swami Year One revolved around Eric not winning, rather than the victory of any one person. For most of the season, the leader was Susanne, who was ten years old and had no football betting experience. (And what does this tell us about betting in general, and betting on football in particular?) However, at the wire, Liz and Susanne ended up in a dead tie and had to not only have a final-week tie-breaker, but a season-deciding tie-breaker, based on the number of penalty yards per team in the Super Bowl.

---

[8] Based on the worst win-loss team record, anyway.

Whew! Go, girls, go.

Final ranking in Year One: Susanne, Liz, Pamela (yes, we all beat the overly-emotional-about-football boys), Eric, and Clark. Liz took the title in Year Two. Eric reclaimed it in Year Three. And it bears repeating that I dethroned him in Year Four and held the title in Years Five and Six. It's getting ugly.

Eric created a monster. His co-workers have become rabid players and his home crew is absolutely insane about the game. We've got a Facebook group, a Google Docs page, girlfriends and boyfriends playing, kids texting on their way home from school to find out the scores, and everyone disputing results (as compiled and calculated in a snazzy spreadsheet by the Momela). Eric can hardly get any work done during football season because of all his co-workers wanting to come by and talk a little Swami every day.

Scoff if you must, but the family that wagers together is tighter than ever. If your last name is Hutchins or Jackson, you are hereby cordially invited to petition the Swami for consideration to join our game.

Oh, and did I mention, I'm the Swami?

TAKE YOUR HEAD OUT OF THE SAND.

My island boy husband, a year or two after the events in this chapter.

Blendering Principle #22: The second best time to talk is when you really need to.

At the end of a harrowing workday for me, my husband told me a story from his childhood as he worked the knots out of my neck and back. The words slipped casually from his lips, belying the emotional impact of the subject:

"I'm sure I've told you about what happened to me in sixth grade?" he asked.

"I don't think so. I'll stop you if I've heard this one before." I assumed a light tone. I didn't know what was coming.

"I didn't tell you about the teacher who took me to his house after school and showed me pornography?"

Whoaaaaa. Bombshell.

No, Eric had not shared this story with me before. Porno for pre-pubescents is not something one easily forgets.

Here's what happened:

At the age of eleven, Eric attended a religious school (which is no longer in existence) on St. Croix. His parents sent him to this particular school, in part, he said, because of the permissive environment of some of the other schooling options, as well as the very public early seventies' "sex, drugs, and rock 'n' roll" lifestyles of several teachers at those institutions.

His secular school employed a young male teacher who was especially popular with the kids. He was fun, "one of them," and sometimes snuck them over to McDonald's at lunchtime in defiance of the school rules.

One day, he invited Eric and a few of his buddies to stop by his house — close to the school — and watch some TV with him. How cool was that? They were singled out; they were special. They went to his home.

We are adults. We know what comes next.

They were children. They did not.

Keep in mind, they were children with good parents, parents like Eric and me, who had warned their kids about situations like these. But children are . . . children.

The teacher served them snacks, encouraged them to look at the array of pornographic magazines spread out on his coffee table, and began setting up his reel-to-reel projector, all the while telling them how as young men they would love the movie he had to show them. He told them that they were really lucky, because most of the other boys did not get to do things like this, but he, their beloved teacher, would share this with only them.

Eric recalls the fear and uncertainty he felt. He didn't dare sneak a glance at his two friends until Mr. Z left the room. Then, they quickly made a pact to offer up an excuse about needing to go home and get the heck out of there.

Time fuzzes up his memory of what happened next, but he does remember that he didn't tell his parents.

Did y'all catch that?

He didn't tell his parents. Neither did the two other boys.

Why? And this is important, so take note: they were afraid of getting in trouble, because they knew they should not have gone to the teacher's house. The "compromising situation" theme is common with pedophiles. They often create conspirators by coaxing children to take tiny steps over line after line, until the child feels too complicit to speak up.

Eventually, they told some friends, and one of those friends told an adult. That adult brought the parents and school into the know, and ultimately the school parted ways with Mr. Z, who then parted ways with the island.

This was obviously not the education the school had hoped Mr. Z was imparting to their youth. The school had no idea. The parents had no idea. Most of the kids were oblivious as well.

Too many of us can relate to stories like these. A strong, beautiful woman of my acquaintance was raped by her friend's father during a sleepover when she was a child. So, as parents, what do we do? How do we keep our kids safe?

One option, with many pros and cons, is home schooling, but this only protects our children from predators at school. Pedophiles don't restrict themselves to schools, although many do seek ways to work with young people. Be careful any time you entrust your kids to others.

It is important to communicate frequently with your kids about this issue and make it safe for them to talk to you. Reward truths when you can, rather than punishing a child's bad choices. We also believe in keeping our kids busy and giving them less mall or cruising time. But this option does not guarantee success, either. No option does. It's a rough world out there.

We decided to sit down with our teenagers and re-discuss the issue. We told them Eric's story. We related it to their lives and activities. And we prayed about it.

"Why didn't you just deck him?" 160-pound, fifteen-year-old Clark demanded, sounding angry but scared.

"We were three ninety-pound kids, and he was a 240-pound adult," Eric explained.

"Still . . ." Clark didn't know how to process the predicament of helplessness Eric's story presented.

There's a blendering corollary to this story. A childhood school pal of Eric's went to prison as an adult for allegedly molesting his teenage stepdaughter's friend. Several years into his incarceration, the girl exonerated him, admitting that it was her own father who was sexually abusing her. She had sought an end to it by means that felt emotionally safer to her at the time than accusing her dad. Eric's friend made it out of jail, but he had contracted AIDS, and died shortly thereafter, penniless and ruined.

Just as it is important to protect our children, it is also important to protect ourselves. Think carefully about your interactions with the youth in your life, especially as a stepparent. Be sure that you do not leave yourself open to dangerous situations. Eric and I never allow ourselves to be alone with children other than our Hutchins-Jackson clan, and we are very careful with our respective stepchildren. We love our kids' friends, but we don't fool ourselves into thinking that we know everything that goes on in their lives, or how that might play out in relation to us.

This issue isn't an easy one. It cuts in all directions, and it's not uncommon. It's no fun to think about, but it's not something we can ignore. Make the time. Do anything but remain silent about these issues with your children and your co-parents.

A TINY TOKEN OF MY DEVOTION

Blendering Principle #23: Keep it real.

One August, Eric and I braved the back-to-school crowds at Target, and Eric picked the checkout line. In all the lines around us, people that had gotten in line after we had were soon signing their charge slips and heading out the door, and we were still languishing in checkout line hell.

"You pick checkout lines as well as you pick movies," I said. He was, after all, the man who had made me see *Nacho Libre* with him in the theater.

"Oh, I think you'll agree this wait was worth it," he replied. He smirked.

"Whaddya mean?"

He gestured with his thumb, and looked a little like Arthur Fonzarelli when he did it.

I craned my neck around the motionless line of humanity in front of us. My eyes landed belly-button level on the voluminous breasts of the cashier. Breasts that hung to her hips. But it wasn't her breasts that arrested my eyes. It was the tattoos on each of them that she displayed above the low-cut scoop-neck of her size XXXXL top. On her right breast, she sported an elongated funhouse-mirror version of Yosemite Sam, who probably started out normal-sized twenty years ago. On her left breast was a similarly distorted Tweety Bird. Each tat had writing below it: a name and a date. By enormous strength of will, I tore my eyes away and back to my husband's.

"OMG," I whispered.

"OMG," he agreed.

"Can you read them?"

"It's a boy's name and date on one, and a girl's name and date on the other."

Just then we heard the person ahead of us ask her about them.

"This one here's for my son, and this one's for my daughter," the cashier drawled. She beamed as she pointed to each.

I know my jaw fell open. Her children. She was displaying commemorative tats on her free-flowing gunnysack breasts of each of her kids.

"That'd be a way to keep Susanne and Clark in line," Eric said. "You could threaten to tattoo their names and faces on your breasts if they screw up during high school."

"Maybe it would be more appropriate to threaten to tattoo one of them on each butt cheek, if they were buttheads," I said.

"Then we could call them buttfaces, and it wouldn't be derogatory," he said.

By now we had reached the front of the line, so we stopped our conversation and held in the giggles long enough to make it to the parking lot.

"I wonder if someone could make temporary tattoos for you like that?" Eric asked. "It would be pretty funny."

I didn't answer. I was already mentally staging the family Christmas photo around them.

Would I lie to you?

Blendering Principle #24: Honesty. Period.

When it comes to raising responsible kids, I am no expert, but Eric and I do have five kids between us. Call us well-practiced, at least. The key principle we live by? Truthfulness. At our house, our kids hear us say super-annoying things like these:

- We would rather hear bad news than no news at all.
- Do you think I would keep my job if I lied to my boss like you lied to me?
- Tell us the truth and we'll reduce the punishment. Lie to us, and we'll find out anyway and raise it.
- If you lied like that to your friends, you'd have no friends.

All of our kids have lied to us about one thing or another. Certainly, young kids go through a phase where lying is common and noncritical, but the stakes rise as they get older.

We reward truth-telling and tackle lying as a "choose to lie, choose the consequences" foul. The worst consequences we can dream up are reserved for lying, and we make sure the kids know about them up front. We tailor the consequences to each child for maximum motivation. Money motivates one, so we take away allowance. Socializing is most important to another; no phone calls or playdates. Screens are the pressure point for the third. You get the picture.

Our system works well with our neuro-typical children. It doesn't work so well with Clark, our ADHD kid. While all our offspring believe they're smarter than us, Clark's grasp of reality is tenuous, and he knows with a moral certainty that he is smarter than anyone on the planet and will never get caught. Add that to the fact that all his choices are driven by an ADHD perspective of life lived in the belief that he has only four seconds left to live. Lie to get his way? Awesome. Any consequences? None that he can see in the next four seconds.

We have to remain accountable for involved parenting, for structuring rules that motivate the kids to be accountable. When we show up earlier than the kids expect us — or when they don't expect us at all — just once or twice, it works wonders on them. Requiring receipts with change, like an employer would, encourages them to be honest. Keeping their friends' parents' phone numbers in our mobile phone contacts makes them sit up a little straighter. And friending all their friends on MySpace and Facebook works, too — over time, they forget we're even there.

One of our kids' friends posted on her Facebook wall before an adult-supervised party we were hosting, "How about we bring the alcohol into the party in water bottles and then your parents will never know?" Except for the pesky little fact that we read it on Facebook, we might never have found out. And that's how we came by the rule of no outside foods or beverages for the party.

All bets are off, though, when it comes to lying and Clark. When our son takes his meds, the incidents of his truth-telling (and helpfulness around the house) shoot up. Without the meds . . . whoa, Nellie. But I'll save any more discussion of that issue for Clark's starring turn in *The Clark Kent Chronicles.*

ADHD or no ADHD, meds or no meds, we'll put up with messy rooms and sleeping late—but not untruthfulness. We believe in choosing our battles wisely, and we wave the white flag on those we strategically choose not to fight so we can win the war of raising responsible kids.

Kids with clean rooms? Not a biggie to me. Kids I can trust? Worth fighting for.

TRUTH OR
CONSEQUENCES

**Blendering Principle #25: Responsibility comes
from accountability, and lack of accountability
comes with consequences.**

Are you living an accountable life? I won't pre-
sume to tell you what you should be accountable for.
You get to decide, and you can keep it a secret. But,
whatever it is, are you living up to it? By that I mean,
do you follow the rules when no one is watching?

I don't believe in this "What happens in Vegas
stays in Vegas" crap. There couldn't be a more
destructive concept to the fabric of our society, in my
opinion. Sure, it's funny. I like funny. But a joke
shouldn't be your moral compass.

Accountability is a bedrock, a foundation, a cor-
nerstone. It comes from within, and it is simultane-

ously individualistic and collective. You can be accountable to your deity, your country, your spouse, your employer, yourself, or, even better, all of the above. Kids can add "to parents and to their schools" to that list.

Okay, I'll dismount my moral high horse now.

I will confess: I am not always 100% accountable. I get lazy. I grow complacent and think no one is watching. Consider parenting, for example. Isn't enforcing accountability with your kids — day in, day out — one of the hardest things to do as a parent? I think it is. We remember them as the precious toddlers they used to be. We want to be the fun parent occasionally, instead of the drill sergeant. We have a 7:30 a.m. client call, so when they walk out the door late on their way to school, we think, "Well, she deserves the consequences the school dishes out," but we don't follow up to make sure there *are* any consequences.

Some days, I'm just so damn tired. As a parent, I am the role model, the motivator, the monitor, the enforcer, and the cheerleader. But I check out occasionally and find my attention to the details, the little "tells," has slipped a notch. I lack accountability for parenting.

I want to raise responsible kids. Kids who follow the rules even when the homeroom teacher isn't turning her attendance roster in to the administrative office. Even when the school isn't handing out demerits for tardies and absences as they rack up.

And so, with that, it's time for me to spill it:

Is she the angel child?

Or the devil daughter?

Here's the voice mail I got one day:

"This is the assistant principal of your daughter's middle school. I'm calling to talk to you about her excessive unexcused absences from homeroom."

WTF?

To my knowledge, she didn't have a *single* unexcused absence from school. Besides, she was an A student, a self-starter, a competitive swimmer; she was the easy child.

Before I called the principal back, I texted Susanne.

"Msg from principal. Do you have unexcused absences from homeroom?"

"Y"

Uh oh.

"How many?"

"idk"

Double uh-oh.

"More than 5?"

"idk"

"When was your last one?"

"I think I went once last week" (Yes, you read that right: she WENT once.)

"What? When did this start?"

"idk"

"Susanne Jackson, did this start a month ago?"

"idk"

"2 months?"

"idk"

This was futile. I left a return voice mail for the principal and emailed her, only to have my email bounce back fifteen minutes later on my first, second, and third tries. I gave up. I called Eric and we plotted strategy together.

Susanne crept in from school at 4:15 that afternoon. She knew what was coming, and come it did. Two painful hours later, we were through the worst of her sobs, and she had made it to her hugging, snuggling recovery phase. I had grounded her for a month and put her on zero tolerance for anything less than exceptional behavior during that time, with one day per offense instantaneous add-on penalties. Susanne is our "social consequences" child—if she chooses a wrong behavior, the only consequence with any impact on her is one that curtails her social life.

I still had no idea how many infractions we were talking about, but it was clear she had knowingly violated school rules multiple times. This is serious in our family. We want to raise kids who follow rules even when no one is looking, and challenge disagreeable rules upfront, by legitimate means. March, protest, plead, write in, or do whatever you want to do to oppose the rule, but if you lose or don't protest, you follow them. Susanne got the "Look at the Ten Commandments, look at our U.S. Constitution, look at your middle school rules" speech, as well as the "You will not drive a car throughout your entire teenage years without me beside you in it if I can't trust you" speech.

Susanne's rebuttal? Homeroom was before first period, and it was just hard to get up in the morning. She wasn't skipping it; she just had trouble getting there on time. Sometimes she had so much trouble, she missed it altogether, poor little dumpling.

Excuse me?

I am here to kiss her goodbye before she walks out the door most mornings. Her explanation could account for a few tardies, but all those absences pointed to a knowing decision to skip.

"I didn't skip any classes, Motherrrr."

Oh, the way a teenage girl can say Mother.

"You skipped homeroom, Susanne. So many times you can't remember how many."

"No, some of them I was just tardy. But anyway, I didn't skip. It's not a real class. It's a waste of time."

Ah, now we were getting somewhere.

It turned out that Susanne — a child whose dominant method of getting her way was passive resistance/ignoring instructions — was getting her way at school, too. She'd started coming in late, and nothing happened to her. She opted not to show up. Nothing happened to her. So she decided to ignore the rules, because there were no consequences.

Or so she thought.

One of my emails made it through the school's firewall after all, so I got this note from the new principal: "Susanne has 32 unexcused absences during Mentor [homeroom] this year, in addition to several excused absences. I would have contacted you sooner, but this was just brought to my attention."

*THIRTY-TWO   THIRTY-TWO   THIRTY-TWO
THIRTY-TWO THIRTY-TWO THIRTY-TWO THIRTY-
TWO THIRTY-TWO THIRTY-TWO THIRTY-TWO
THIRTY-TWO THIRTY-TWO THIRTY-TWO THIRTY-
TWO THIRTY-TWO THIRTY-TWO THIRTY-TWO
THIRTY-TWO THIRTY-TWO THIRTY-TWO THIRTY-
TWO THIRTY-TWO,* my mind screamed.

*Oh my God! I should have grounded her three times as
long!* I added a blog series to her punishment. Nothing is feared more in our household than to become
blog fodder. I also added a summer of weekly
volunteer gigs at an animal shelter.

Once we had her consequences squared away,
my mind turned to a critical question. How could the
school have let thirty-two go by? Had the homeroom
teacher ever turned in attendance? If not, how did
they now know the number? If the teacher did keep
attendance, what was she thinking?

Well, Susanne knew she was supposed to go to
the office of her own volition and get a demerit for
each unexcused tardy, and the school's procedure
was to assign discipline based on the number of
demerits. School policy called for a detention after
four, full-day in-school Saturday detention after
eight, and suspension after twelve.

Susanne did go for demerits . . . four times. She
got one detention. After she got a detention, she quit

going for the demerits, but didn't quit skipping out on—excuse me, BEING TARDY TO (Talk to the hand, Susanne)—class.

Meanwhile, the teacher continued to take attendance, but never followed up or followed through. Or if she did, nothing was done in the office. Until the new assistant principal arrived. Thank goodness for a fresh set of eyes.

Had they enforced their policy, they could have nipped Susanne's behavior in the bud. I'm disappointed that we all didn't get that chance. She's too young and headstrong to be allowed to think she can sneak this by everyone. As it was, she went months thinking that breaking the rule thirty-two times didn't matter. But breaking a rule thirty-two times matters in real life. If you don't believe me, skip work thirty-two times, shoplift thirty-two times, or cheat on your spouse thirty-two times, and watch what happens when you get busted for all of them on the thirty-second time. It ain't gonna be no first infraction then. Even before you're caught, each instance tears a tiny hole in the fabric of your character. It matters.

Per Susanne, the principal informed her via a "you are the luckiest girl in this school" chat in the hallway that they would assign her two additional demerits, bringing her total up to six. So, Susanne was about to get a free pass on twenty-six of her thirty-two tardies/absences from homeroom. Even though in all likelihood she would have stopped as soon as she had been caught, Susanne *knew* she was breaking the rule in all thirty-two instances; it was almost no consequence at all to her to be charged for two of them at this point. Yes, she was grounded at home, but still. It didn't seem like the school expected much accountability from her. Was this a "learning message"? If so, we feared Susanne was learning she could get away with murder when she felt like it.

The real message: Just be cute and sneaky.

Who was dropping the ball on accountability? Who was accountable in the first place? IMHO, all of us:

- Eric and me as parents, to set the rules and actively hold Susanne accountable to them — spot-check her, ensure that she is where she says she is, and pay attention to those nagging little doubts that creep in.
- My child, to follow the rules, *whether anyone is watching or not.*
- The teacher, as an employee of the school, to follow and enforce its rules (and the same for any administrative employees involved).

- The school, to monitor and enforce their own rules and hold their employees accountable, and to be accountable itself for upholding its standards and mission — to Susanne, to us, and to all the other parents and students at the school.

That's a lot of accountability there.

So where did that leave us in this incident? To my way of thinking (which is greatly influenced by my hybrid status as an employment lawyer and human resources consultant), if the school failed to hold the teacher and staff accountable for taking attendance, shame on the school. If the school and the parents failed to enforce accountability with Susanne, shame on us both.

We're holding Susanne accountable by giving her a healthy dose of consequences at home; that's our responsibility, and we accept it.

Letting Susanne get away with only two demerits wasn't even enough to earn one detention or push her to the next level of their progressive discipline policy. Really? The school was gonna let her slide?

So I did something unthinkable. I asked the school to hold my child more accountable. I asked them to reconsider increasing the consequences to her.

They reacted with shock.

Was I really the first parent in the history of this middle school to make this sort of request? I hoped not. I was serious: I didn't feel I could afford to let them show my impressionable daughter that she could escape accountability to the school. Mama on a rampage. Mission: Hold my child accountable.

We asked the school to give her a Saturday full-day detention. The assistant principal thought I had lost my mind. In a good way. Yay! They gratefully granted my request, and I sent Susanne off with a to-do-at-detention list of extra-credit activities. (Picture her rolling her pretty blue eyes here.) The school also gave her a well-deserved U for unacceptable conduct.

Lessons learned? Oh, so many about our child and our complacence, but the biggest lesson I learned is that there are administrators out there who are willing to help us create responsible adults, but we need to support them. Ours were so conditioned to parents whining that their little precious angels didn't deserve detention that they didn't even try to give Susanne one. They expected us to give them flak since they had failed to follow their own rules.

But their failure shouldn't excuse Susanne's behavior entirely. I don't think it would have been fair to suspend or expel her, but she should not have gotten away with nothing. And it turned out, the principal thought so, too.

I have a friend whose daughter's teacher – of her own accord – reversed a parental discipline decision. My friend had prohibited her daughter from participating in a class Valentine's party. The teacher thought that was too harsh a consequence for the child, and let her attend anyway, without talking to the parents. While I think it's important that kids maintain a positive association about school when possible, I think it is even more important for parents and teachers to support each other's decisions, or communicate when they cannot do so.

Yes, our kids are precious little angels, but they should reap the (age-appropriate) consequences of their actions, or they will become irresponsible and unlikeable adults. I'm here to raise kids to adulthood, not win popularity contests.

Yay school, yay principal, yay Saturday detention!

(And boo Susanne Jackson – you are still in big trouble, kiddo.)

DON'T BURY THE HATCHET IN YOUR EX'S BACK.

**Blendering Principle #26: Embrace the positive.
Release the negative.**

Good things can happen for the kids when ex-spouses bury the hatchet. Everybody wins.

When Edward and I divorced, we did it in bitter acrimony, like almost everyone does, even the so-called amicable or best-of-friends Hollywood divorces. Some are bitterer than others, but most of us emerge from divorce hurting. And mad. And embarrassed. And scared. Whether of being alone or of failing again, we are scared.

I look back on the year or so after my divorce, and I wish I could take back a few of the things I said and did. I fanned the fire of my ex's anger, and I showed my own in front of my children. Only a few times, but that was more than enough.

I am proud, though, of the ex-spouses we have become. Even at our worst, we talked about the best interests of the children. We disagreed on what that looked like, but we disagreed on everything for twelve years, so why would things be any different then? But we each decided (and I intentionally use the word *decided*) to believe that we were both acting in what we sincerely believed was the best interests of our two kids. If that were true, then at worst, we only disagreed. Ours was not a battle between good and evil.

It still took us two years and a lot of money to finalize a custody agreement. Okay, so what. We got there. Life goes on.

This chapter would be a lot more exciting if I shared the list of things I regret. I'm not going to go there though, for two reasons. First, because it would be unfair of me. Second, because I believe that what you focus on is what you see, and I don't want to cause any of you to focus on the negative. Instead, I want to tell you the things we did right, the positives, and the result we achieved in the end.

Things We Did Right

1. We always assumed that whether we agreed with each other or not, the best interests of our shared children came first to both of us.

2. We talked respectfully about each other and our new significant others in front of the kids . . . with a few slip-ups in the beginning, and apologies to the kids and to each other in front of the kids after the slip-ups. Yes, to each other.

3. We attended the same events, separately, to show united support of the kids. Even when it made us uncomfortable, even if the other spouse brought their new partner, because the kids were more important than our feelings.

4. We included each other in all aspects of our children's lives. We shared emails, report cards, pictures, and, occasionally, anecdotes. We co-parented. We sought support on major issues and ensured we agreed or could amicably disagree.

5. We learned to wish each other the best. We for-gave. And, over time, we forgot a lot.

My best girlfriend and her ex were not able to do these things. A comparison of my little sociological experiment in ex-co-parenting to hers is interesting. Edward made it okay for my kids to love my husband, to talk about him, and to show affection for him. But my friend's kids were put to a continual loyalty test, where to do less than dislike and disparage their new stepfather was high treason. My kids' relationship with my husband is fantastic. My friend's kids' relationships with their stepdad is strained, at best.

By no means are we perfect. I don't love Edward, and sometimes I don't even like him. There's still anger there if I look below the surface and dwell on the negative. I daresay he would say similar of me. But anger is self-indulgent in this circumstance, and to allow myself the luxury of focusing on my feelings does my children no favors. I've done it. At my worst, I still do. But I always regret it and refocus on the positive.

I love the advice a mentor once gave me: "Do the behavior and the attitude will follow."[9] I believe it. I

---

[9] Thanks, Eric Allenbaugh. You can read more about him at http://www.allenbaugh.com.

did the behavior of positive co-parenting long before I felt positively toward Edward, but in time, the attitude of positivity followed the acts of positivity.

The side benefit? The more I focused on the positive and did the behavior of respectful co-parenting, the more I forgot about the past. Focusing on my kids helped me move on and heal. Win-win. We certainly didn't do it perfectly, but we did it right enough that we are proud of the results. We've allowed our kids to blend with their new stepfamilies.

Maybe now his mother will forgive me for divorcing her son?

Nah, probably not.

THIS HURTS ME MORE THAN IT HURTS YOU.

When I married my first husband, I didn't know two things: He had ADHD, and our marriage would end after twelve years.

I'm not sure what impact the knowledge of either fact would have exerted on my choices in the year we married, but the fact is, marriage and parenthood involve lots of future unknowns. The past is certain. I had a beautiful son, Clark, in 1995, and he has ADHD. His father and I split up years ago.

Edward and I divorced because of our own issues, but like any couple that endures a difficult time with a child's disability, we lived under more pressure than we had expected when we said "I do." We will never know whether our marriage would have been easier if we'd made different decisions about

Clark's diagnosis and treatment when he was very young.

Yet isn't it always something? Marriages will always face adversity, because people will always face problems. It's the human condition. Edward and I, like any couple, faced a variety of challenges. In the end, we simply decided we didn't want to go through life together.

Our divorce raised new issues. We would continue co-parenting our children together. But how? Neither of us wanted to deprive the kids of time with the other parent, nor the other parent of time with the kids. But I worried about Edward's inconsistent parenting, especially when it came to Clark. And Edward worried about my frustration over and inability to understand Clark's ADHD. Two years into the divorce, we agreed to trust each other and stay flexible. This worked well for a few years. Until it didn't.

Hold that thought.

The divorce had an immediate positive impact on Clark. Nope, I'm not living in a dream world. The divorce broke his heart, and it had some expected negative impact, but it also helped him. Clark hated conflict and he couldn't tolerate raised voices. Picture him as a small child running away from our angry, fighting voices with his hands over his ears, slowing down to flutter his left hand and run in a circle, then resuming his flight. Divorce meant that the conflict was over. Full stop. Big sigh of collective relief.

Another benefit to him was that my frustration with his ADHD was no longer exponential. I stopped feeling angry at Clark because he was acting like Edward. I know now that this played a role in my feelings before the divorce.

Since then, Edward and I have done the best we can to split parenting time and duties equally. I think this makes us somewhat unique — so unique, in fact, that we confused our attorneys and the judge. But we wanted to send a clear signal to the kids that we love them equally and believe in the other parent's abilities.

How does this custody arrangement work in practice? For starters, it requires us to live within walking distance of each other. This is not a divorce book, so I won't bore you with the mundane issues, like how I preferred never to see my ex again, but I still have to run into him at the Kroger every week.

I'm kind of kidding.

Our custody arrangement works fine for Susanne, our neuro-typical daughter. She's organized and navigates the weekly transitions with ease, if not always with a perfect attitude. Some weeks she whines, "I don't want to go back and forth," but I'm lucky. Even when it isn't my week, she comes over after school and pesters me (in the best possible way) while I work until Edward comes to pick her up after work. It's the blessing and the curse of having a home office.

That arrangement never worked as well for Clark. He has enough trouble organizing himself in one space, and transitioning week by week was hard for him. We tried to set up environments in each home that required him to tote as little as possible back and forth, but the stuff that tripped him up couldn't be duplicated. Did he have his worksheet from algebra? Today is a robotics day — did he leave his shirt at the other house? It was clear that the strain of preparing to transition, transitioning, and failing in the transition stressed him out. From day one, I petitioned his father for a primary space for Clark at my house, but Edward, understandably, didn't want to give up the time with him.

Until high school, when he came to me with tears rolling down his face. The time had come to let Clark live at my house and spend every other weekend with Edward. It was a painful decision for Edward to make, but he did it in the best interests of his child.

That never could have happened if we hadn't buried the hatchet. And thank God. Clark needed it. As Edward explained to Clark and me, he has ADHD too, and his was not the better household for Clark. He concluded that he could do best for Clark by giving him stability and stillness at La Hacienda de Hutchins. Clark was elated. He adores his father, but he hated the stress.

So, how did the change go? Well, awesome, really. Clark is still Clark Kent the WonderKid, and he still has ADHD. But our collective stress level plummeted. We have far fewer fire drills, running back and forth between houses trying to determine where he left or lost his homework, his clothes, his meds. He does his work in the same place at the same time with the same rules and same supervision every day. He suffers under the eagle eye of his very non-ADHD momma, which means an endless stream of prompts:

"So Clark, what do you think you should do next? And then? And how about now? Did you write it down? Could you write it down? If I begged you on bended knee, would you consider writing it down? Would you just pretend to write it down so I could have a moment of peace? Thanks."

I'm very happy.

And so, it seems, is Clark.

FOR THE LOVE OF SUSANNE

Kids. Sometimes you either gotta love 'em or kill 'em.

Susanne needed to practice applying make-up for her theater class. Silly me, I thought make-up was supposed to improve my looks. But, no. Susanne applied the aging technique to me. I looked like Brünhilde on a bad day.

What could possess me, a vain former beauty queen, to allow myself to look like this? Only the best of reasons. I did it for the love of Susanne.

Don't worry. It washed right off.

THE WHISPERING
HUTCHINS

**Blendering Principle #27: We aren't all the same.
Deal with it.**

You know how there are sounds only dogs can hear, like police whistles? Well, at our house, not even the dogs can hear the voices of Eric and Liz. *Even the Bionic Woman could not hear them*, y'all. I call them the Whispering Hutchins.

At first, I thought it was just me. Maybe I was deaf from growing up as one of the hollering Fagans. Or listening to too much rock music. Worse, I thought they only whispered around me. Did they secretly mock my distraught face and complete lack of comprehension?

"Ha, she has no idea what we're saying," they might say, and slap a conspiratorial high five.

Surely not, but it reminded me of a nasty little game my ex used to play. He would mumble inaudibly to someone, and when they asked him to repeat himself, he would hyper-enunciate in a bellow, "DOES SUCKING D*CKS MAKE YOU DEAF?!?!?" The listener usually felt pretty stupid, if not offended (or both). Oh, he got laughs, but they were uncomfortable ones. With my husband and stepdaughter, I felt stupid at best, and like the butt of a bad joke at worst.

I can hear my husband if it is just the two of us nose to nose. He thinks I crave intimacy when I rub my face against his—hell, all I want is to understand one damn thing he's saying. I can't rub noses with Liz, so I'm out of luck with that girl.

For several years, I would say one of a couple of things in the wake of the "hrmplkeja mhrisyaoiijh" under their breath:

- What?
- Can you repeat that?
- I'm sorry, but I can't understand you.

It annoyed me to say it, and I suspected it annoyed them worse to hear it and repeat every single word to me. Hence, my conclusion that in order for them to endure this for years on end, it had to be intentional.

Except that I've noticed *no one else can hear them either.* I can't tell you how much it delights me when someone like my mom asks me under her breath if I understand a word either of them are saying, as she smiles brightly at them with a blank look in her eyes. I nod sympathetically when Liz's friend confides he can't hear her most of the time. I chortle when Eric's co-workers bemoan the same issue. I am positively giddy when the waiter at the Flying Dutchman in Kemah asks Liz to repeat her order three times, and then looks up blankly until one of us takes pity and amplifies it for him.

It's not just me! Woo hoo!

Still, I worried. The "what, huh?" repetitions weighed on me. I felt guilty.

I gave up. I quit asking for do-overs. I reasoned that if the issue bore repeating or explanation, they'd find a way to get their point across. If I couldn't understand them, I smiled and ignored them.

Well, Eric didn't like this solution. Liz, a teenager, didn't notice, but Eric did. We went back to the game of "Say it, ask for a repeat, say it again." But I'd played one too many hands of this game, and it was time for a big change or fifty-two card pick-up.

So, I got my !@#* hearing checked. First, I did a number of different types of hearing tests online. Next, I evaluated my ability to hear others. I spent a few weeks writing down any time I could not hear people well enough to understand them, other than the Whispering Hutchins. The list was short: zero people. Then, I conducted an official test with an ear, nose, and throat doctor. And what did she say?

She said my hearing was completely normal. That it was, in fact, A-plus. That it's not me. I have no hearing problems at all.

She's wrong, though.

I do have hearing problems. TWO OF THEM. And there ain't no hearing aid, bull horn to the ears, or cattle prod to the behind that will solve them. But I love them anyway. And I'm getting a whole lot better at reading lips. In fact, I think I can read Eric's now

. . .

In Praise of Swim Teams and Stepdaughters

Blendering Principle #28: Effort + Repetition = Success.

So far, with two of five offspring in high school, one in college, and two graduated from college, we are either remarkably lucky or remarkably successful. Our kids get into the normal kinds of trouble, but they achieve higher than average successes, by the standards of the Western world. My husband and I have trod paths similar to theirs. Of the seven of us, six have been on swim team, and five swam hardcore at some point.

Coincidence? I don't think so.

A friend recently pointed me to Malcolm Gladwell's book, *Outliers: The Story of Success*, and asked me if it matched our experiences. Gladwell writes that family, culture, and friendship each play a role in an individual's success. He notes that success "is not exceptional or mysterious. It is grounded in a web of advantages and inheritances, some deserved, some not, some earned, some just plain lucky."

Granted, Eric and I are not churning out the type of outliers that Gladwell profiles, like Albert Einstein, Bill Gates, and the Beatles, but nonetheless, our kids are more successful than most, and people notice. And I believe there's something about the swim team life that encourages a kid's success.

First, I submit that it is an advantage to be raised by parents who deliberately create an environment that will maximize each child's chances of success, and who look for activities that build life skills and help ground the child amidst the dangers and distractions of the growing-up years. You probably wouldn't be reading this book if you didn't believe this was a parent's responsibility.

My parents strove to create this for me. I in turn strive to create it for my children and stepchildren, because I believe I am accountable to provide this for our offspring, that it is my privilege and my duty.

Now, with this in mind, let's look at the life of my stepdaughter Liz. (Although I could just as easily talk about her talented older sister Marie, or maybe even Susanne, although the final results aren't in with her yet.) Liz has participated in year-round swim team since she was five years old, and before that, watched Marie swim competitively. She has played a variety of other sports and engaged in activities ranging from an elite choir to flute to yearbook. Between her high school's swim team and her private swim team's schedules, she had to spend fifteen to twenty hours in the water every week. That was added on to her normal high school class schedule. Liz had a 3.6 grade point average. She was a Texas 5A Regional Finalist in the 200-meter butterfly. She represented the U.S. Virgin Islands at the Caribbean Islands Swimming Championships in Cuba in the same event. She was a member of her high school's award-winning and prestigious Concert Chorale group. By just about anyone's standards, Liz has succeeded.

How did swim team play a part in her success? Despite the number of hours it required, or maybe because of it, Liz was able to fit everything in. She knew she was time-constrained, so by necessity she and other swimmers became masterful from a young age at organizing their lives. Swim team did not always require so many hours of her; the hours increased as she climbed to higher levels of competition. So, at the same time Liz swam in high school, thirteen-year-old Susanne spent only ten-plus hours in the pool each week, in comparison to Liz's fifteen-plus.

Liz, without any parental prompting, packed her backpack and—most nights—two swim or school bags, her lunch, and her snacks, and laid everything out before bedtime. She left the house at 4:45 or 7:15 each morning, depending on her practice schedule. She did not return home before 7:20 p.m. She couldn't run home if she forgot something, and both Eric and I worked, so she had to plan for what she needed or do without. She got ready, sometimes more than once a day, in tiny, crowded bathrooms or locker rooms. When she arrived home at night, she quickly ate and showered, did homework, and tucked into bed. Her early rising, long days, and high level of athletic activity required sleep, sleep, sleep. To give herself more time for sleep and homework, Liz voluntarily took summer school so she could have a study hall period during the school year. Not too shabby.

Part of enabling success is ensuring that teens stay out of trouble, and swim team contributes to this goal beautifully. Liz had a nice social life, but she was too sleep-deprived to get out of hand, even on the weekends. And she and her swim team friends prized their membership on their club team, whose coach was a stickler. He wouldn't tolerate kids that were drinking, doing drugs, or too tired to practice because they were out partying all the time. They were normal kids, and we assumed there was a little more fun going on than we knew, but not a whole heck of a lot.

The swim team environment is a culture of achievement. The swimmers are all striving for their personal best, and they normalize the effort required to achieve it for each other. People, if you have never done it, I can't begin to tell you how difficult it is to swim a 1500 for a warm-up, fifty 50s each at a pace I can't make for a single 50, and another 1500 for a cool-down. Or how excruciating a 200-meter butterfly really is, how much your shoulders hurt, how hard it is to breathe. Yet it becomes normal for these kids to do this, because they look around them and everyone is doing it.

Normalization of effort. Normalization of sacrifice. Normalization of achievement. But it takes a village of coaches, teachers, and parents, in addition to the kids' effort.

Participation in this type of life-skill-building activity demands sacrifice on the parents' part. For years, we have made the twenty minute drive to and from the pool multiple times a day. Before Liz got her driver's license, between her and Susanne, we drove eleven to fifteen round trips every week. Most swimmers cannot compete at high levels without dedicated parents and without the training and support of their club team, which costs a couple thousand dollars a year. (Some teams offer scholarships or are able to discount their fees if they are supported in whole or part by donations.)

Swim meets range from two to three days apiece, and with two swimmers in the house, we usually had two meets a month. Eric and I have sat on concrete decks for hours upon days cheering the girls on, because our support was critical to their commitment and ultimate success. They needed to know we cared and were watching them, or they would disconnect from the activity. So we watched. And we watched and we watched and we watched!

Success, of course, is not just about effort and achievement. It is also about quality of life. If your child hates an activity, then it's probably not adding to their quality of life. If they enjoy it, if they love it, if it adds instead of subtracts, this is a success.

Liz loves to swim. The first thing she does when we visit a hotel with a pool is grab a swimsuit and run for the water. She loves swimming so much that she continued swimming in college. She plans to combine swimming with a little bicycling and running someday, too, and follow in her dad's footsteps to triathlon. In fact, Liz wants to swim so badly that when she qualified for CISC in Cuba and we realized that our funds had run dry, she chipped in $400 of her own savings, gave up part of her birthday and Christmas haul, and initiated (with our help) a fundraising campaign for the $2000 she needed. She raised it, too.

What would our life, and hers, be like without swimming? More sleep, probably! But other than that, I can't think that it would be better. I believe that the swim team experience in our household follows the *Outliers* mold. It has created life skills in our kids that add to all the other advantages, accidents, and efforts that contribute to their successful upbringing.

Three cheers for swim clubs.

Hip, Hip, Hurrah!

Hip, Hip, Hurrah!

Go swimmers and stepdaughters!

Schoolworkin'

Blendering Principle #29: It takes all kinds of people and all kinds of minds.

Five kids equals worry times five about school-work. But most of our worry has been for naught. Four of five of the kids excelled no matter what we did. They got into scrapes and scraps and tight spots, but their grades were super. And then there's Clark.

Clark is an eternal struggle for us, God love him. With Clark, the struggle is to keep his personal traits—namely, ADHD coupled with a well-centered personality, which finds very little need to push itself and is nearly impossible to motivate—from sabotaging his gigantic brain. This causes him to stand out in a family of type-A, athletic, academic, and professional overachievers. The boy marches steadfastly to his own syncopated beat, although he floats more often than he marches.

So, in his freshman year at a 3,000+ student public high school, young neuro-atypical Clark insisted that he be allowed to try to a) Take pre-Advanced Placement classes for all his substantive subjects, and b) Succeed or fail independent of parental control. We said yes to both. It was definitely time for him to fly solo—so said his counselor, his doctor, and his parents—even if he had to take summer school as a result.

Each grading period was a battle to the death to overcome zeroes for missed assignments and low grades on assignments that hadn't piqued his interest. He failed science in grading period one and moved out of pre-AP; he almost failed geography in grading period two, and then he failed English and geometry in grading period three, with a 61% and 59% heading into the last two weeks.

This was a new experience for us. A new and painful one.

I have to share, though, some wonderful emails from his English teacher, who seemed to see the real Clark. She wanted to keep him in her class despite my desire to move him out of all the pre-AP classes in hopes of a less stressful household.[10]

For your reading ease, I've put the email thread in chronological order:

***

————-Original Message————-
From: Ms. B
To: Pamela Hutchins
Subject: Clark's English grade

I just want to make certain that you have been checking GradeSpeed for Clark's current average. He has really slipped, as his current average is 61. I just spoke to him about this. He said it was the homework sentences. I'm concerned about his average. He said he will need to take the final exam early, which is fine with me. I asked him to come one day when he can devote time to study before this final; he should make it a day when he does not have other difficult finals to take. Just let me know the day. He needs to do well. He is a very smart young man and should be doing much better. Let me know if you have questions.
Ms. B

———————————————

[10] I'll admit it, the person whose stress I was most concerned about was my own. Clark was unperturbed, except over my intermittent and voluble frustration.

————-Original Message————-
From: Pamela F. Hutchins
To: Ms. B
Cc: Edward Jackson, Eric Hutchins
Subject: Re: Clark's English grade

Thank you, Ms. B. We are painfully aware. We have battled exactly this type of performance since kinder-garten—big brain doesn't translate to classroom, but does get a little better every year, and certainly his ADHD struggle makes it no easier. We have rein-forced the need to do extremely well from here on out and to seek out help, and he has chosen a day for his test where his other class is PE. He really wanted to take the pre-AP classes, and finds them so much more interesting than his normal classes, but we are really leaning toward regular classes at the semester, as we are always on the brink of disaster. He does enjoy your class, and we really appreciate your communication and concern.
Pamela Hutchins

————-Original Message————-
Ms. B wrote:

I would hesitate to put him in the academic level. Of course, that is your decision, but from my experience in teaching that level, the atmosphere is not always conducive toward higher-level thinking. I have several

students for whom I would encourage such a change, but Clark is not one of them. Of course, Clark has to be willing to put forth effort, and if he is not, he will not be successful at this level. Thank you for your kind words and your support.
Ms. B

————-Original Message————-
From: Pamela Hutchins
To: Ms. B
Cc: Edward Jackson; Eric Hutchins
Subject: Re: Clark's English grade

Thank you. We have never found anything positive or negative that truly motivates Clark, so whether he will choose to put in the work is the big question. He has said he will come to tutorials for the next two weeks. I hope he shows up. Could you please confirm whether he attends? The closest things we have found to motivational for him are A) Interest, and B) Texas A&M admission. If you notice anything that appears to be working, let us know! :-) Have a good last few weeks before break—it's crazy times, I'm sure!

————-Original Message————-
From: Ms. B
To: Pamela Hutchins
Subject: RE: Clark's English grade

I'm sure grammar does not inspire his interest, and as a faithful Longhorn, A&M anything is out of the question. He appears to have enjoyed *The Count of Monte Cristo;* I'm afraid *Jane Eyre* may not be as entertaining. I'll see what I can do if you decide to leave him in here. I will let you know if he comes next week. Enjoy your holidays as well.

Ms. B

***

What's so special about this email string to me? Clark's teacher took the time to inform me about what was going on, to get to know my child, and to gently encourage the parent as well as the student. To me, it shows a woman doing her job, plus a little bit, which is more than we could ask for, especially in a gigantic public school and with a student like Clark, who could drive a teacher out of the field completely.

All our kids went to private school for at least the first six years of their grammar school education, some of them more. But I'll take your private school teachers and raise you an overworked, underpaid public school teacher, and I'll come out ahead. And I'll sell you Clark if you'd like.

And oh—Clark stayed in her class. And he passed.

CHRONICLES OF THANKSGIVING

Blendering Principle #30: Give it time, and meanwhile, give thanks.

So what's a blendered Momela thankful for?

In our new household, Year Two, and as a graduate of Texas A&M, I was sooooo thankful that A&M played a respectable game against my law school's alma mater, the University of Texas, rather than making us sit through what I feared would be the Thanksgiving Day Massacre. I was also thankful that Clark did not wear his Aggie chef's[11] hat to this game . . . and to my parents for the great tickets . . . and to

---

[11] Yes, you read that correctly. A towering chef's hat, a la Cordon Bleu Cooking School, but in maroon with the words "Texas Aggies" festooned in white embroidery across it.

our dear friends for a wonderful Thanksgiving dinner.

But what I was especially thankful for was spending a quick visit with my delightful in-laws, Larry and Beth, and our nephew and niece in Jacksonville. I was getting to know them and believed that they saw the type of wife I was and parents Eric and I were to their grand- and stepgrandchildren.

It hadn't started that way. The road was paved with misinformation about me before I entered the family. I was an anomaly and a pariah. I was a visceral reminder that Eric had divorced his first wife, that he was the only one in his family to divorce. I put a scarlet D onto Eric's and my breasts. I was the possibility, in their eyes, that he would shirk his paternal responsibilities. I was the mirror in which no one on either side of our family wanted to view their own marriages.

The first time I welcomed Eric's parents into my home, his mother's pain crushed me. The weight of it bore down on us so heavily that it was hard to lift our forks to eat the food I had prepared, but I mustered up all the cheer I could. By the end of the evening, Larry assured me I had won his heart. It meant the world to me, but I knew I hadn't won Beth's yet.

Over time, Eric and I got the chance to show Beth our marriage and our co-parenting. Each visit with her grew lighter. I knew she loved me for Eric's sake. But it wasn't until we brought Liz to live with us that she began to love me for mine.

I suspect I would have felt much the same as Beth. I'd love to say Eric had an easier time with my family, but I can't. In my family, my mother embraced him first, but it took Eric years to forge a real relationship with my father and my brother.

And in Eric's family, it wasn't just his parents who struggled. No one knew how to treat me, or even what to call me. When my brother married his wife, it was an automatic that we instructed our kids to call her Aunt So-and-so. When I married Eric, his brother and sister-in-law instructed their kids *not* to call me Aunt Pamela. They decided that Ms. Pamela was more appropriate. This would have hurt in and of itself, but learning that they had also coached them to call the maid Ms. Something-or-Other, yet called the other brother's wife (and Eric's ex-wife) Aunt dug a deep pit of pain in my heart. I zipped my lips and lifted my chain, literally and figuratively. And the niece and nephew called me Aunt Pamela within fifteen minutes of my arrival anyway, on that Year Two Thanksgiving.

At the end of that visit, Larry put his warm hand on my arm, and he gestured Eric in close.

"You two, you warm my heart with the way you love each other and all the kids. I'm so happy for you, and I'm so proud of you. You're good people, good parents." He patted me.

Eric and I wiped our tears away and hugged Larry and clutched each other. We both craved his approval. We needed it. So, yes, I had that to give thanks for, that clearing of major hurdles in the obstacle course of our life, and many other blendery and non-blendery things as well.

I was grateful that my stepson Thomas ended his week on a high note, and was crossing my fingers for good things to happen for him, and soon.

I was thankful that our children were healthy, happy, and showed that they loved me.

I was thankful for how easy my relationship with Marie had become.

I was really thankful for my company and all of its consultants, employees, and clients. And for Eric's company, too.

I was grateful that I'd had the opportunity to write and finish a manuscript. I was appreciative of the staff at Multisports Health Center, and of my body for taking me many, many miles on my feet, my bike, and through the water.

I was thankful that my parents were (and are) my best friends, besides Eric.

I was thankful for seeing *The Blind Side*, which was a wonderful movie about some really great people. I celebrate the times I can take my family to a well-made, engaging movie with a message of positivity and accountability.

I was most thankful, a million times thankful, for Eric, who inspires and supports me, who loves me and allows me to love and adore him back. I am thankful for the things I can do because of and with him, and for all that we share.

And did I mention that I'm thankful that the Aggies didn't get their ass handed to them by the Longhorns?

POETIC JUSTICE

Blendering Principle #31: The universe abhors a vacuum, and in all things seeks balance.

poetic justice, noun: The rewarding of virtue and the punishment of vice, often in an especially appropriate or ironic manner.[12] *A literary device. Think "What goes around comes around."*

justice, noun: Fair treatment and due reward.[13]

Justice v. poetic justice — the key difference is irony.

Earlier, you learned that our precious Susanne had skipped or been late to homeroom thirty-two

---

[12] Thanks to www.thefreedictionary.com.

[13] More thanks to www.thefreedictionary.com.

times. Even though the number later fell to twenty-three when we compared the dates to her excused absences, we still found her lack of commitment to the rules troubling. This incident followed an F she received in band one grading period for not following those rules, either.

Many punishments ensued in our pursuit of justice and learning. We grounded her, she performed slave labor at home, I wrote about her on *Road to Joy*, we asked the school to increase her consequences by requiring she attend a Saturday detention, and she did community service.

Imagine our surprise when the band director who had given her an F the previous year selected her for his elite thirty-member band the next year—the top band in her performing arts magnet middle school.

Surely he'd made a mistake?

Nope.

The director forgave her rebellion in favor of her talent and improved behavior. Lucky kid. She responded beautifully to his faith in her. I couldn't believe she was the same surly girl who'd begged to quit flute last year. But was this justice?

We decided to call it the just result of a miscreant fully punished and rehabilitated.

Our next surprise came when she learned which teacher she would have for history class that year: it was the homeroom teacher she had manipulated and abused so shamelessly the last year. Someone must have paired Susanne with this teacher deliberately to see her squirm. And squirm she did, but she still wrote an apology-and-pledge note to her teacher, promising perfect attendance and attitude for the year. (Possibly at the behest of her mean mom.)

In response to my inquiring email about Susanne's attendance and behavior, the teacher wrote, "So far, super-fantastic in both regards."

Huh? Could we even be sure this was our daughter? (Well, it had only been three weeks.) I believe this particular pairing of teacher to student was a small serving of poetic justice for both of them.

Susanne also learned that the school had stuck her in an "enrichment class," a special program for those needing a lot of extra help in academics, even though as a pre-AP student she needs little help. This was due to a conflict in her schedule that prevented her from taking one of the classes she really wanted.

Methinks this is another side dish of poetic justice for her bad behavior.

But a champion came to her rescue. The principal who had called me at home to report Susanne's truancy the previous May maneuvered Susanne into a journalism graphics class, which became her favorite one. I appreciated the principal volunteering to help, and I am satisfied that this result is just, in light of Susanne's post-malfeasance rehab program — even though I am the same woman who called for her own daughter's head when the school didn't want to take it.

The final sign of her successful rehabilitation into responsible eighth-grade society, and the main course of poetic justice the universe served her?

The attendance counselor asked Susanne to be her aide.

Susanne started working in the attendance office every day for one hour. The kicker? She loved it. And the attendance counselor loved her. Go figure.

Parenting lessons learned: Your kids only say they'll hate you forever when you ground them, put them on work detail, ask their school to put them in Saturday detention, and write about them. The universe often provides the perfect consequence.

And the teachers and administrators at her school are the best.

Justice demands one last punishment: publication of this photo.

There. Now I can completely forgive her for the whole twenty-three-skipped-classes incident.

The ultimate in "what comes around goes around": Susanne is my own flesh and blood. Every time she curls her lip into that adolescent snarl and backtalks me in that beeyatchy voice, I hear my mother yelling at me through her tears. "I hope you have a daughter just like you someday, Pamela."

Well, I did. And there is no one happier about it than me. Except for maybe my mom.

ROCKIN' 'N' ROLLIN'

"So, I'm thinking we should all sign up for the San Antonio Rock 'n' Roll Marathon this fall and do it together," Marie said, a portrait of nonchalance.

We were sitting around watching ESPN together at my parents' house. Her comment was apropos of nothing, although earlier Eric and I had told her about completing our third marathon in three months and earning our prized Texas Triple windbreakers. And I may have droned on about ultra marathons and trail running for an hour without a breath.

Marie had never completed a marathon—or a half marathon or any other running race—but she was a world-class recently retired swimmer. She had once trained for a few months for a Half Ironman triathlon. She ran regularly, but not distance. And she was a junior in college. Marathons are not the activity of choice for most twenty-one-year-old girls. Even though I ran distance from the age of fifteen, I partied too hard at her age to run marathons.

Not Marie. Marie was our serious child. She was in the prestigious Honors Humanities program at the University of Texas. She'd swum endurance events from her early teens. And at seventeen, she had founded a non-profit to help in the fight for better education for the youth of the Caribbean. So maybe a marathon wasn't such a big surprise for a girl like her.

"Wow, sure, yes," Eric and I stuttered.

Within minutes, I had signed us all up online. I shared our training program with Marie. She would train in Austin, we would train in Houston, and never the twain should meet until San Antonio in November.

That summer, I convinced Eric to attempt a trail ultra, the Rocky Raccoon fifty-miler, scheduled for the following February at Huntsville State Park. We decided the Rock 'n' Roll marathon with Marie would fold nicely into our training schedule for the big event.

We are both given to extremes. Obviously.

So we changed our game. We moved our runs from asphalt to dirt. And crushed rock. And caliche.

And gravel. To mud. Sand. Grass. And, unfortunately, to hummocks, hillocks, dips, depressions, bumps, stumps, stones, and holes.

Each week, our Sunday "long runs" topped fifteen miles and counting. Years of floppy ankles caught up with me. I torqued and twisted them, especially the right one, over and over. Scorching white-hot pain plagued my instep. And it migrated. My instep still hurt, but soon the base of my foot hurt, radiating back to what felt like a railroad spike through my heel.

My father didn't raise no sissy. Mind over matter. More Aleve. I kept going.

The month leading up to the Rock 'n' Roll sucked.

Marie kept in touch. Her training was spotty, but she still felt she could do it. We hid our troubles from her.

Eric spent all of October in Canada for work. His hours and six-day work weeks made training tough. An ankle sprain didn't help. The weather turned wintery and he got sick.

I trained alone back in Houston. The week before the Rock 'n' Roll, I did a solo marathon at a five-hour training pace on concrete along Buffalo Bayou in Houston. The pain in my right foot was nearly unendurable. I stopped every six miles and texted

Eric a photo. One thousand miles away, he ran his marathon in a state park near the Bay of Fundy, snapping and texting pictures for me. We finished together. He flew home the next day.

Between coughs on our drive home from the airport, we compared notes.

"I don't think you should do this race, Pamela. I think you need to go to the doctor and figure out what's wrong with your foot," Eric said.

"You're one to talk, sick boy with the sprained ankle," I retorted, ignoring his advice.

"I have no business doing this marathon," he said.

"Nor do I," I said.

"So are you gonna scratch?" he asked.

"Are you out of your mind? My college-age stepdaughter asked me to do a marathon with you guys. I would run across nails to do this."

Eric smiled. "Yeah, same here."

And so the next week, we lined up at the start with a sweetly nervous Marie, and off we went. It was my worst marathon finish ever. It was slower than my training runs. I had ugly mood swings, as the pain rocked me and I lashed out at everything around me. Eric held my hand when the waves came over me, probably to keep me from swinging at anyone. It made an impact on some spectators, though. We saw the same people several times during the course, and they always yelled, "Look, it's the couple that holds hands while they run."

I won't tell you about how awful it was. Instead, I will tell you the truth: It was wonderful. It was a parenting and athletic top-rung experience. I wouldn't trade my fastest runs on my fittest days in the best of conditions for that death march with Marie.

It was hard for all of us. Marie learned about the twenty-mile wall and the death shuffle of the last six miles. She experienced the humiliation of seeing an old, limping fat woman pass her. Of the rock 'n' roll bands finishing their set and packing up before you reached them on the back of the course. Of porta-potties never being around when you needed them. She discovered that training counts, but heart matters more. We all suffered together in the unseasonable heat and humidity. But we finished. Almost together. In a streak of expected competitive spirit, Marie passed us one minute before the finish line. Gotta love that in her.

Blendering Principle #32: Shared success is so much sweeter than solo.

So, Congratulations to my rockin' stepdaughter Marie for completing her first marathon in San Antonio! She was glowing. It really is a wonderful, wonderful feeling to cross that mental threshold and know you CAN do it. She did it again two years later, one hour faster. Marie kicks butt.

And me? Well, I didn't run again for eighteen months after that day. My pain had a name: Plantar fasciitis. It hurt to turn Marie down the next few times she asked us to race with her. I've healed by now, and I run distance again, just a little more carefully and on even ground.

But I would endure the pain in San Antonio a thousand times again for the thrill and satisfaction of completing that race with my husband and step-daughter. Top ten Momela moment.

13,161 FEET HIGH

I had my Momela marathon moment with Liz, too.

Remember the rocking blender-bonding of the trip to Maine, to the house that held a special place in the hearts of Liz and Eric? That was their place. My place was my grandparents' farm. My kids' place was New Mexico, in the vacation home of my parents, Liz's blendered grandparents.

We introduced Liz to New Mexico in Year Two, but in Year Three we had the chance to take her there without any of the other offspring for the changing of the leaves, with the complete attention (whether she wanted it or not) of Eric, my mom and dad (GiGi and Poppy), and me. It's always fun to have the kids in a group, but as with Marie and the marathon, our pinnacle moments are when we can pull one of them away from the pack.

By this time, Liz had come to think of New Mexico as her place, too. It didn't replace Maine, but it was part of her bundle of benefits in the blendered family. Liz had also come to think of Poppy and GiGi as her grandparents. Sometimes it's easier for her to embrace them as her grandparents than it is for her to accept me as her stepmom. This makes sense; I represent a direct threat to her relationship with her mother. I understand this. I try to work around it.

At the time of this trip, Liz had only days before she'd celebrate her sweet sixteen birthday. She was a junior in high school, and she idolized Marie. After consulting Eric and my parents on potential activities, I suggested to Liz we make the eighteen-mile hike from Red River up to the summit of Wheeler Peak. At 13,161 feet, Wheeler is the tallest mountain in New Mexico. There are shorter routes to the top, but since my teens it has been our family tradition to climb Wheeler the long way, once a year. Did you expect anything different from us? It probably wouldn't surprise you by now to hear that my father has climbed several of the Seven Summits. After eight back surgeries. But I digress.

Liz jumped at the opportunity to become part of the family legend.

We grownups hid our grins. Our kids think we do these types of things with them for exercise or to see the scenery. They have no idea the plotting, scheming, and planning (ah, yes, planning, lovely planning) that goes into our efforts to solidify our family unit, to give them memories, and to develop them as little humans. Like that country song, "And she thinks we're just fishing."

The day started crisp and lovely. We sandwiched the beautiful Liz into the middle of our pack and proceeded to talk her ear off for the next eight hours. For every landmark, there was a family story that she now shared in and added to. We saw eight bighorn sheep, a first for all of us. We chanted "How many rocks could a rock chuck chuck," and laughed about the rock chuck that bit GiGi's hand when she fed it a sandwich, years ago. Liz learned about us by doing what we did, and she taught us about her as she bore down and climbed the last thousand feet, oxygen-deprived and exhausted. We shared the high that comes only from standing at the top of the world.

Liz's eyes sparkled for days afterward as she shared the tall mountain tale with her friends back in Houston.

"What did you do last weekend, Liz?" they asked.

"Oh, nothing. Just climbed the tallest peak in New Mexico."

"NO WAY," they would say.

Oh, yes. She did.

Because that's what we do in our family.

REFRIGERATED CHILD PORN

Remember Dolly Parton's song "Coat of Many Colors"? When our fourteen-year-old daughter decorated cakes for Halloween, I opened my refrigerator to this sight:

I called Eric over. "What the heck do you think that is?" I asked.

"That's a cake with twelve penises," he said.

"That's what I thought. Cake of Many Penises. Like the song."

"I've never heard that song."

Eric obviously has led a sheltered life. I snapped a photo.

"Is that picture for your Mother of the Year application package?" he asked.

I ignored him. Duh, of course it was. I'm a total shoo-in.

I called Susanne.

"What are those things on top of your cake, hon?" I asked, pointing to the sagging brown mounds of icing.

"Haunted trees in a haunted forest. You know, like with no leaves."

"They look like haunted penises," Eric piped in.

"NO!" Susanne said. Her face turned crimson.

"Did you see Susanne's penis cake?" Clark asked as he walked through the kitchen.

"STOP!" Susanne cried, but now she was doubled over, sides shaking, hands over her face with a smile peeking out each side.

"OMG, Susanne, you're like an erotic cake decorator," Clark's friend Ying Ying said.

Yeah. We're so proud. Either she's a very talented sculptor . . . or not.

She offered to pay me not to include this picture in this book. I absolutely draw the line at taking payola from my kids. I have standards, you know.

Clark's girlfriend Allie also had a cake in the fridge.

Clearly, that's a pumpkin patch. Not a penis in sight. Maybe I could swap out daughters?

Nah. That Susanne's pretty darn cute.

Wutliss

Fully blendered. Who wouldn't want to be part of this Wutliss[14] crew?

---

[14] Phonetic Cruzan pronunciation of "worthless." However, note the beers are O'doul's. We're not THAT much fun.

DEAR TIM TEBOW, ONLY YOU CAN SAVE MY DAUGHTER.

For those of you I am about to offend, I apologize in advance. But the following is a somewhat accurate transcription of actual events at our house. Sort of. So, don't be a hater; I love God, I love Jesus, and I dang sure love me some Tim Tebow.

***

Dear Tim Tebow:

I'll bet there's a lot of pressure on you already, what with you being the Broncos' quarterback, building third-world hospitals and all, and inventing Tebowing. I really hate to add to the stress, I do, but Tim Tebow, only you can save my daughter.

We've done (almost) everything right with 15-year old Susanne, but you know how precarious morals and behavior are in a girl this age. For awhile, we had her wearing a WWJD (What Would Jesus Do) bracelet as a reminder of how to act. Then she discovered live boys, and a dead Jesus, even a risen one, just didn't completely cut it anymore.

We've seen signs she may be headed down the wrong path. When she was in seventh grade, she had twenty-three unexcused absences to homeroom, and it's possible she was selling drugs or committing sins of the flesh when unaccounted for. Another time she didn't return her leftover lunch money at the end of the week, and I am pretty sure that breaks one of the Ten Commandments, but I'd have to look it up. Also troubling are her attempts to emulate Angelina Jolie.

I think that's the worshipping false idols, right? Anyway, I saved the worst for last. At Halloween, she made a cake decorated with twelve penises. I don't know where that one falls vis a vis the Commandments, but I know that it is bad, really, really bad.

Things have improved lately, and this is where you come in. Last month, Susanne announced that she was marrying you, Tim Tebow. My husband and I discussed the possibility, and we want you to know that, while she is still a little young, you have our blessing. However, in the meantime, we assume you would like her to graduate from high school with virtue intact and no criminal record.

To that end, we have a new and effective strategy to control Susanne's more wayward behavior. Let me give you an example. Last night, I asked her to set the table and was aghast at her response:

Me: Sweetness, would you please set the table for our sit-down family dinner, and be thinking about what you are thankful for, for when we say grace.

Susanne: Mom, I don't have to set the table. I'm going to marry Tim Tebow and be really rich and have a maid to set the table. I'm thankful for that.

You see what I mean? So then I prayed about it for a while, and that's when I received what I took to be a message directly from God: only Tim Tebow can save my daughter.

So, I said: Susanne, I haven't met your fiancé personally yet, but from everything I've read, I believe he would want you to honor your mother. I'm concerned about the impact of your behavior on your upcoming nuptials.

Susanne, eyebrows raised: Huh?

Me: Please, Susanne, set the table and make Tim Tebow proud of you.

Susanne, flipping her hair: Make Clark do it.

Me: Susanne, Tim Tebow wants you to set the table.

Susanne, with her hand up: Whatever.

Me: What I meant to say, Susanne, is that Tim Tebow told me to tell you to **set the @#$%* table. Right now**. And I'm not kidding.

And you know what? She did. I'm really pleased with the positive impact you have on her; I think that's the kind of relationship any parent would hope for.

Right afterwards, I snapped this photo:

I think it's a sign.

If you can resurrect the 1-4 Broncos and bring them to the playoffs, I feel certain you are strong enough to save my daughter.

Thanks in advance.
Your future mother-in-law,
Pamela

p.s. Please, God, forgive me for telling my daughter that Tim Tebow used the word @#$%*.

p.p.s. If things don't work out between you and Susanne, Tim Tebow, I have two more daughters.

Blendering Principle #33: Encourage appropriate role models.

THERE ONCE WAS A MAN FROM NANTUCKET

And now, for comic relief, a demonstration of why I write prose rather than poetry: odes to my husband and three youngest kids, in limerick style. I framed these for them one Christmas. They were not impressed.

1. Liz "Bean": Our high school swimming teenager with more clothes, shoes, makeup, and hair straighteners than the rest of us put together.

> There once was a girl from Bellaire
> Who daily did straighten her hair
> A fast-swimming teen
> A Facebooking Bean
> She can never decide what to wear

2. Clark: The Dallas Cowboys' biggest fan. I couldn't limit myself to just one verse here.

> There lives here a boy named Clark
> He treats school much like a lark
> If he ever gets through
> What he's started to do
> We are sure he will leave quite a mark

> A dramatic and unruffled soul
> A haircut a lot like a bowl
> Witten's best fan
> Homework not in his plan
> To be a big dork is his goal

3. Susanne: Our middleschooler whose hygiene habits indicate she is not yet interested in boys. Her loves are dogs, swimming, and disagreeing.

> Susanne Marie is her name
> Contrariness is her main game
> She's strong and she's tall
> She likes dogs best of all
> But her showering skills are quite lame

4. Eric: And then there is my long-suffering island-boy-turned-Texas-redneck wannabe triathlete hus-

band, who puts up with me posting his most embarrassing moments on my blog, *Road to Joy.*

> There once was a man from St. Croix
> With a fanny as fine as a boy's
> I may give him heck
> But I love his red neck
> He inspires the name *Road to Joy*

WAFFLING

At nearly fifteen years old, Susanne had never had a boyfriend. Well, she hadn't if you didn't count her year-long engagement in kindergarten to Nicholas Crouch. Or her rebound relationship in first grade with Jackson Galleon. Since then, though, she has had no boyfriends. She's plenty boy-crazy and at 5'7" with blue eyes and long blond hair she is totally gorgeous (and wears a bigger bra size than me, WTF), but she's saving her heart for Tim Tebow.

Or so we thought.

Recently we were staying at a Red Roof Inn on the outskirts of San Antonio. Based on the horse trailers and Chevy trucks, most of the other guests were cowboys, or something like it. Susanne's fallback position if the whole Tim Tebow thing doesn't pan out is to marry a World Champion Rodeo

Cowboy. Runner-up will do if he has the biggest truck.

Susanne preceded me into the lobby one morning for the free breakfast. Just as she sashayed in the door, a booted, scruffy young man of the presumed cowboy variety was making his exit. He had a good ten years on her, but that didn't dim the gleam in his eyes that glinted off his ginormous belt buckle. I locked him in my mama-death glare as I stepped quickly in behind my little filly.

Meanwhile, Susanne's eyes had lit up, too. *Oh no*, I thought, ready to move between the smitten cowboy and my seriously-underage daughter. The words, "Put your tongue back in your mouth and step away from the adolescent," were forming on my lips, when Suz turned to me.

She whispered excitedly, "They've got those waffle makers shaped like Texas!!" And then, because she is my daughter after all, she bolted for the food bar.

Looks like Tim Tebow is safe for now. But I'd better warn him never to get between her and breakfast.

I CANNOT TELL A LIE.

How do you explain a family like ours in what is supposed to be a hardly-truthful totally-feel-good Christmas letter—a Southern tradition I dutifully follow? This is what our blended family Christmas card looked like one year.

***

Some of us have called ourselves family longer than others. Some used to call us family and now don't. But whatever, whenever, and whoever, we are us. From all of us at our house, Merry Christmas to you.

We are celebrating our fourth Christmas as a Hutchins-Jackson household. Well, technically, it's the fifth year, but we added one more Hutchins about a year into the timeline, so we'll call the first year "Year Zero." Yeah, it's confusing. Deal with it.

Anyway, here's a five-picture Holiday Card Retrospective.

So, the big question is, How did the year treat us? What silliness will I now regale you with, pretending only the good stuff counts? Well . . . all in all, I'd count it a success.

We started out and ended with five offspring. One of them is mad at us, but that's not unusual. Usually, in fact, several are at a time. One is heading back to graduate school, another graduated from college. One earned the first F in the family and skipped class twenty-three times, and another followed up with a feathered flock of FFFFFs on his fall report cards. One is about to graduate high school and another is about to graduate middle school. One quit football but discovered debate. Another scored a car and a boyfriend. It's been up down and all around. Fun. Crazy. Sad. Happy. Awesome.

Eric and I continue our fiery "there are no words for it" wonderful marriage. Seriously, pinch me. It's that good. (A moment to reflect on everyone that said we would never last. One word: wrong!)

His job is solid and he loves it. We both wish he traveled less. Someday.

My job is solid and I am grateful for it. We both wish I could write as an occupation instead of an avocation. Maybe someday. :)

We acquired a little place we call Shangri-La in Nowheresville, Texas, where Eric discovered his inner Bubba-mon and we installed our Quacker travel trailer. We visit as often as we can, and we have purchased our house plans. Someday.

We still can't sell all the property we own in Lancaster, SC. Buyers, anyone?

Our athletic pursuits took a nose dive. Me: Plantar fasciitis. Him: work, travel, and health issues. We are determined to regain our triathlon mojo in the upcoming year.

I rewrote my first two novels several times. I wrote a third novel. I have agents circling (pray). I started a blog called *Road to Joy* about utter nonsense that thousands of strangers read for God knows what reason. *Nice to meet you* I write for three other blogs, too. Oh, my.

Liz signed a letter of intent to swim for Adams State in Alamosa, CO, while juggling the demands of choir.

Clark has taken Cross-X debate on the National Champion Bellaire High School debate team by storm and has his eyes on state, and he was the videographer for the varsity football team.

Susanne plays flute in the honors symphonic band at her magnet performing arts middle school, and she swims at a high level, too.

We're very proud of them. And they're teenagers. So, we battle teenage girl mood swings, the "I want" syndrome, ADHD, social media, social lives, and we try to get a straight truthful answer out of everyone. I'd get in more trouble than I could get out of with the three of them if I gave you the details.

We are just like everybody else and nothing like any of them. And we love it. Feel free to read more sometimes-true tales of our adventures at **http://www.pamelahutchins.com**. Or not and say you did. Whatevs.

Just know that in our corner of the world, t'ings is good, mon, even when they're not.

Merry Christmas and Happy New Year, y'all.

***

And that's how it's done.

AND THIS EXPLAINS WHY OUR DAUGHTER ENDS UP AN EXOTIC DANCER WHO TELLS HER THERAPIST, "IT'S ALL MY MOTHER'S FAULT."

I hate being sick, especially when my husband is sick, too. Everything gets derailed -- my diet, work, writing, exercise, and parenting. Not that my teenagers required as much parenting as when they were little, with Suz self-sufficient at school, Clark with a drivers' license, and the oldest three outta-da-house altogether. They required a whole lot of other stuff, though, like money, patience, money, money, and more money.

This particular sick week one of them also required attendance -- ours. Susanne had a choir concert. Eric and I strive to attend all of our kids' events. That's why my butt is errantly numbed from sitting on hard bleachers at multi-day long swim meets.

There was just no way to swing Susanne's concert this time. Our guilt was magnified by the weeklong trip we'd made to Chicago to see Liz sing, but what could we do? Our attendance would risk infection of 100 choir members and their assembled 750 fans. And we felt, and probably smelled, like hammered dog poo, too.

We drove Suz to the concert together in solidarity (and in case one of us passed out from fever), and I wrung my hands the whole way.

"Are you sure you are OK with us missing this, sweetie?" I asked.

"MOM, it's fine. I don't want you to go. Have you looked in the mirror? You haven't brushed your hair in a week," she said.

I turned to Eric. "Does this make us bad parents?"

Eric doesn't pass up many opportunities to raz Susanne, even when he's on death's door. "It'll give her something to talk about with her therapist someday."

Susanne rolled her eyes in his general direction.

I loved this game and joined in. "Remember MadLibs last night? That prophetic story that had her as an exotic dancer? She'll be at her therapist and go, 'I was all set to be a veterinarian for starving animals in third world countries and marry Tim Tebow, when my parents quit coming to my choir concerts. It's then that I turned to drugs and became an exotic dancer.'" I blew my nose.

"Mo-o-o-o-m," Susanne protested, with her hand over her mouth. She doesn't like to be caught smiling.

"I noticed she used a heavy hand with the poppyseed dressing tonight at dinner," Eric added. "She made a point of telling us that opium comes from poppies. And I think that was right after you said we couldn't go tonight, on the heels of us bagging on her for the Blake Shelton concert."

"And me missing my duet with Blake of God Gave Me You," I lamented.

Susanne had taken two friends in our place. Methinks she was happy with the spoils of flu last night. Still, she rubbed a little salt into the gash in my heart. "Hey, I videotaped it on my cell phone for you. Did you hear him calling you to the stage?" Hair toss. "I didn't think so."

Eric ignored the sidebar. "Next thing you know she'll be asking us to grind hemp seeds onto her strawberry toaster strudels."

I dropped my Blake woes and rejoined the fun. "Shave mushrooms over her macaroni and cheese," I said.

"Huh?" Suz asked.

Eric's voice was starting to give out, but he rasped on. "Pour cough syrup into her Dr. Pepper," he said.

"She'll start stealing our Sudafed, and her room will always smell like a freshly cleaned um[15]," I said, then rattled the Malibu with a cough.

"And to think it all started because we had the flu," Eric sniffed, wiping his dry eyes with a pretend hankie.

We pulled to a stop to drop off our daughter.

"You look pretty, honey. Sing good," I chirped.

Susanne just shook her head, but this time she didn't bother hiding the smile. "You guys are weird."

She shut the door and joined her friends walking into the church, three young ladies with the world in their hands, beautiful in long black satin dresses with full length black gloves.

I put the car in drive. Tiny guilt prickles bit along my arms and face again. "Do you think she really will rat us out to a therapist some day? What if she

---

[15] And if you get that inhalant reference, you grew up in the same era I did.

repeated this conversation, for instance? Maybe that's where we're bad parents and missing this concert isn't the real problem. Or maybe I'm delirious on too much Theraflu and Mucinex."

Blendering Principle #34: Just do your best. It will be good enough.

Eric leaned his head back against the passenger seat and sighed. "Relax, Mom. I'm pretty sure she's going to turn out just fine."

LEAVING A PIECE OF OUR
HEARTS IN COLORADO

So back to that beautiful teenage girl, Liz, who graduated from high school in chapter one. It seems fitting to circle back to her now.

Three months after watching Liz cross the stage to accept her diploma, we loaded up the Suburban for another cross-country family road trip, this time with her maroon Jeep Liberty in caravan. Liz, Clark, Susanne, Eric, and Pamela, awake before dawn and racking up the miles and memories together again.

The day before we left her in Colorado, Eric and I took a Suburban-load of college freshmen to Wally World to buy supplies. We squeezed 6'2" little Clark and 5'7" baby Susanne in the third seat, and they hung on every word the college kids had to say.

The new Grizzlies (their college mascot) were getting to know each other. They swapped stories from their childhoods and family lives.

A familiar voice rose above the din.

"One time, we all went to Maine together in this same Suburban. Two weeks, all of us, eating sandwiches. It was SO COOL," Liz said. "We went to our grandparents' cabin on Lake Mooselook, and we stopped and took pictures at every single state line with our stupid armadillo."

Eric and I grabbed each other's hands. Our eyes met. This was it. This was that moment. The memories she shared with her new friends, they were our memories together. We had done it.

"And then another time, we climbed a 14,000-foot peak in New Mexico. It's two hours from here. We can go to that cabin on the weekends. Let's climb Wheeler together," she chattered on.

And so it went, until we had to leave her there, the girl who is not my daughter. She is my stepdaughter, which is plenty good enough for me to proudly claim her. And her sister and brother.

Fully blendered, we were now one child lighter back in Houston. And a little heavy at heart. What better proof did we need that our little experiment was working? That despite our best efforts to screw it up, our kids are blendered, they thrive, they rock?

None, I think. They are perfectly imperfect, as are we.

And I wouldn't change a thing.

ALL BLENDERED

You've done it! You made it through the whole book. Now that you're at the end, it begs the question, though, "What the heck was it she just said?" I usually feel the same way at the end of a book myself. To help you past this awkward moment, here are all the blendering principles for you, in one convenient and easy-to-reference list.

You're welcome. And happy blendering!

1: It's hard to get anywhere if you don't know where you're going.

2: Your mom was almost right: Do unto others as *they* would have done unto them.

3: Culture is everything.

4: Live your plan.

5: Pick your battles very carefully.

6: Bloom like mad, no matter where you are planted.

7: Make your stories legends with heroes and fire-breathing dragons.

8: Laugh together. A lot.

9: Rotate the spotlight.

10: Expect people to exceed your expectations.

11: You never regret the extra mile.

12: Row in the same direction.

13: Celebrate together, every chance you get.

14: Lead by (good) example.

15: Someone always moves your cheese. Get over it.

16: Everything in its own time and place.

17: Make health and wellbeing a visible priority.

18: Help me help you.

19: Flexibility is the key to air power.

20: Facebook is FOREVER.

21: The best time to talk is when you don't have anything particularly important to talk about.

22: The second best time to talk is when you really need to.

23: Keep it real.

24: Honesty. Period.

25: Responsibility comes from accountability. Lack of accountability comes with consequences.

26: Embrace the positive. Release the negative.

27: We aren't all the same. Deal with it.

28: Effort + Repetition = Success.

29: It takes all kinds of people and all kinds of minds.

30: Give it time, and meanwhile, give thanks.

31: The universe abhors a vacuum, and in all things seeks balance.

32: Shared success is so much sweeter than solo.

33: Encourage appropriate role models.

34: Just do your best. It will be good enough.

Excerpt: *Love Gone Viral*

BRING ME A BUCKET.

When people tell me and my husband that we make them want to puke, we gaze into each other's eyes and say, "Thank you!" Then we go home and make sweet, sweet love, while singing each other Marvin Gaye songs and weaving promise rings out of sea grass and clover.

It's hard work, being this nauseating. The effort involved in all this damn smiling — you wouldn't want to take it on, I promise. Totally exhausting. Add to this burden our perfect children and our perfect careers, and you've got the makings of chronic fatigue syndrome, at least.

As my youngest daughter would say, "Whatever."

The first time an acquaintance told me, "Y'all are just so cute together it makes me want to puke," I wasn't sure how to take it. It sounded like a compliment, but it felt like a barb. I thought about her sterile marriage to a nice but unaffectionate man who didn't seem to find her interesting, and about how she laughed about him behind his back. I analyzed the green look in her brown eyes; I'd seen it in other people's eyes when I was with my husband. I concluded that, given the choice, I'd like to keep my relationship over hers, thank you very much. Also, while she seemed envious in a grudgingly admiring way, I'd never seen evidence that she worked to improve her own marriage. Not once. Did she think pukeworthiness just happened by accident, by a sprinkling of pixie dust? I don't believe it does.

So, yep, I am the lucky princess with the fairytale marriage. But I'm willing to bet even Cinderella and Prince Charming had their issues. Unfortunately for my prince, I habitually and publicly confess my more interesting failings, which inevitably involve our relationship from time to time. I guess that in addition to being half of a couple who makes you want to puke, I have diarrhea of the mouth (and fingers), too. Totally irresistible, I know.

I wish I could make it sound more scintillating than it really is, maybe write about how Eric is a compulsive gambler and I am a gender-reassignment success story, and the neighbors have called the cops to break up our fights on three separate occasions. That would be exciting, but it wouldn't be true.

The truth is boring. The truth is that we are as flawed as the next couple. I adore my almost-perfect husband, who puts up with me writing about him and being a gigantic pain in the ass. I love my normal, fallible kids and stepkids[16]. I love our messed-up, wacky life. But just because we adore and love each other, it doesn't mean the rest comes easily.

While I have no scandalous revelations for you, I can share the secrets of how two highly emotional, self-absorbed, over-committed Type-A losers at marriage (we are both each other's second spouse) manage our relationship into the true thing of beauty that it is.

And I do mean manage.

---

[16] I'll refer to family members, friends, and clients from time to time. Names have been changed to protect the innocent — which Eric and I are far from.

(Are you choking on that vomit yet? Stick around.)

If my day job counts, I am a so-called expert in human relations. As a hybrid employment attorney/human resources professional and consultant, I get paid to help grownups manage their workplace relationships. The HR principles I apply at work are, in theory, principles for humans anywhere—like humans in a marriage, even a second marriage like mine.

There's a good reason doctors don't usually treat family members: when it comes to our loved ones, our rational selves are replaced by emotional creatures. Things get personal. Things get messy. All the psychological training in the world couldn't guarantee that someone (and by someone I mean me) will play fair.

Physician, heal thyself. HR Consultant, you too.

So it is with some embarrassment, and hopefully a bit of humility, that I will share our foibles and our feats. We understand how wrong we each got it on our first ride on the marriage-go-round, and we believe that through painful trial and error, we've finally gotten a grip on the brass ring. We know the statistics: over 40% of first marriages end in divorce

and up to 67% of second do, too. The big issues —
emotional intimacy, mutual support, compatibility,
respect, sex, and money[17] — get even trickier when
you add stepparenting, alimony, child support, ex-
spouses, and the "It's easier to say 'I quit' the second
time" phenomenon. But we're beating the odds, and
we want you to, as well. And so we begin. Keep your
Pepto-Bismol handy.

---

[17] And, these days, I'd have to say that technology, like
social media and smartphones, makes these issues more
immediate and drives up the intensity.

THERE'S NOTHING UNDER THE CANOE, HONEY.

This is how we roll.

My husband and I went on our honeymoon in Montana in June, which unbeknownst to us was still the dead of winter. (We hail from the Caribbean.) At the time, we were training for a Half Ironman triathlon,training for a Half Ironman triathlon, so we needed to find an upper-body strength and aerobic substitute for swimming during our two weeks of bliss. Without taking the weather into account, we'd decided that canoeing or kayaking would suffice.

So off we traipsed from Houston to Montana, where we stayed in an adorable bed-and-breakfast near Yellowstone, which we picked because the owner advertised healthy organic food. The beets, quinoa, and cauliflower kugel we were served for breakfast weren't exactly what we'd hoped for, but we felt fantastic. And hungry. Very, very hungry.

Our "Surprise! We're vegetarian!" B&B sat near a tundra lake. For those of you who have not seen a tundra lake, imagine a beautiful lake in a mountain clearing surrounded by tall evergreens. Picture deer drinking from crystalline waters, hear the ducks quacking greetings to each other as they cruise its glassy surface. Smell the pine needles in the air, fresh and earthy.

And then imagine the opposite.

A tundra lake is in the highlands, no doubt, but the similarity stops there: no trees, no windbreak, no calm surface, and no scenery. Instead, it's an ice-chunk-filled, white-capped pit of black water extending straight down to hell, stuck smack dab in the middle of a rock-strewn wasteland. Other than that, it's terrific.

Maybe it was because we were newlyweds, but somehow Eric intuited that I would love nothing more than to canoe this lake in forty-degree weather and thirty-five-mph winds, wearing sixty-seven layers of movement-restricting, water-absorbent clothing. Maybe it was because we were newlyweds, but I somehow assumed that because he knew of my dark water phobia and hatred of the cold (anything below seventy degrees), I was in good hands. My new husband assured me this lake was perfect for tandem canoeing.

So . . . we drove across the barren terrain to the lake. Eric was bouncy. I was unable to make my mouth form words other than "You expect me to get in that @#$%&&*$* canoe on that @#$%&&*$* lake?"

I promise he is smarter than this will sound. And that I am just as bitchy as I will sound. In my family, we call my behavior being the bell cow, as in "She who wears the bell leads the herd — and takes no shit from other cows."

Eric answered, "Absolutely, honey. It'll be great. Here, help me get the canoe in the water. I'd take it off the car myself, but with that wind, whew, it's like a sail. Careful not to dump it over; it's reallllly cold in there. Not like that, love. Where are you going? Did I say something wrong?"

I responded by slamming the car door. Anger gave way to tears that pricked the corners of my eyes. I stewed in my thoughts. I knew I had to try to canoe. I couldn't quit before I started. We were training, and if I didn't do it, Eric wouldn't do it, and that wasn't fair of me.

I exited the car. Eric was dragging the canoe out of the water and trying to avoid looking like a red flag waving in front of me.

Super-rationally, I asked, "What are you doing?"

He said, "Well, I'm not going to make you do this."

"You're not making me. I'm scared. I hate this. I'll probably fall in and all you'll find is my frozen carcass next summer. But I'm going to do it."

My poor husband.

We paddled clockwise around the lake in the shallows, where the waves were lowest, and I fought for breath. I'm not sure if it was the constriction of all the clothing layers or actually hyperventilation, but either way, I panted like a three-hundred-pound marathoner. It would have scared off any animal life within five miles if you could have heard me over the wind. Suddenly, Eric shot me a wild-eyed look and started paddling furiously toward the center of the lake.

"You're going the wrong way!" I protested.

"I can't hear you," he shouted back.

"Turn around!"

"I can't turn around right now, I'm paddling."

"Eric Hutchins, turn the canoe back toward the shore!"

And as quickly as his mad dash for the deep had started, it stopped. He angled the canoe for the shoreline.

"What in the hell was that all about?" I asked.

"Nothing, love. I just needed to get my heart rate up."

I sensed the lie, but I couldn't prove it. My own heart raced as if I had been the one sprint-paddling. For once, though, I kept my mouth shut.

The waves grew higher. We paddled and paddled for what felt like hours, but made little forward progress against the wicked-cold wind.

"Eric, I really want out of the canoe."

"We're halfway. Hang in there."

"No. I want out right now. I'm scared. We're going to tip over. I can't breathe."

"How about we cut across the middle of lake and shave off some distance? That will get you to the shore faster."

"I WANT TO GO THE NEAREST SHORE RIGHT NOW AND GET OUT OF THE #%$&(&^%#@% CANOE."

Now I really had to get out, because it was the second time I'd called the canoe a bad name, and I knew it would be out to get me.

Eric paddled us to the shore without another word. I'm pretty sure he thought some, but he didn't say them. I got out, almost falling over into the water and turning myself into a giant super-absorbent Tampax. He turned the canoe back over the water and continued on without me. This wasn't how I'd pictured it going down, but I knew I had better let him a) work out and b) work *me* out of his system. Looking like the Michelin man, I trudged back around the lake to the car and beat him there by only half an hour.

By the time we'd loaded the canoe onto the top of our rental car and hopped in, we were well on our way back to our happy place. Yes, I know I don't deserve him. I don't question it; I just count my blessings.

That night we dined out — did I mention we were starving to death on broccoli and whole-wheat tabbouleh? — to celebrate our marriage. Eric had arranged for flowers to be delivered to our table before we got there. The aroma was scrumptious: cow, cooked cow! Yay! And, of course, the flowers. I looked at Eric's wind-chafed, sunburned face and almost melted from the heat of adoring him. Or maybe it was from the flame of the candle, which I was huddling over to stay warm. What was wrong with the people in this state? Somebody needed to buy Montana a giant heater. We held hands and traded swipes of Chapstick.

He interrupted my moment. "I have a confession to make. And I promise you are really going to think this is funny later."

Uh oh. "Spill it, baby."

"Remember when I paddled us toward the middle of the lake as hard as I could?"

"I'm trying to block the whole experience out of my mind."

"Yeah, well, let me tell you, sweetness, it was about ten times worse for me than you. But do you remember what you said about falling in, yadda yadda, frozen carcass next summer, blah blah?"

I didn't dignify this with an answer, but he didn't need one and continued without much of a pause. "Well, you were in front of me, breathing into your paper bag or whatever, when I looked down, straight down, into the eyes and nostrils of a giant, bloated, frozen, very dead, fully intact, floating ELK CARCASS."

"You're lying."

"I am not. It was so close to the surface that if you hadn't still had those tears in your eyes, there is no way you wouldn't have seen it. You could have touched its head with your hand without even getting your wrist wet."

"No, you did NOT take me out on a lake with giant frozen dead animals floating in it." A macabre version of Alphabits cereal popped into my mind.

"Yes, I did," he said, and he hummed a few bars of Queen's "We Are the Champions."

"Oh my God. If I had seen it right then, I would have come unhinged."

"More unhinged. I know. I was terrified you would capsize us and then you would quadruple freak out in the water bumping into that thing. I had to paddle for my life."

He was right. I let him enjoy his moment; I'm glad he confessed. But I will never canoe on a tundra lake with Eric again. Even if I got my courage up, he would never invite me.

Cinderella, eat your heart out.[18]

---

[18] There's video of the tundra lake and other parts of our Montana trip on my YouTube channel, The Land of Pamelot. Sorry, there is no video of the elk.

ABOUT THE AUTHOR

Pamela Fagan Hutchins lives, loves, laughs, works, and writes in Texas with her husband Eric and their blended family of three dogs, one cat, and the youngest few of their five offspring. She is the award winning author of many books, including *The Clark Kent Chronicles*, *How To Screw Up Your Kids*, *Love Gone Viral*, *Hot Flashes And Half Ironmans*, *Puppalicious And Beyond*, *Saving Grace* and a contributing author to *Prevent Workplace Harassment*, *Ghosts!*, *Easy To Love But Hard To Raise*, and *Easy To Love But Hard To Teach*.

Pamela is an employment attorney and human resources professional, and the co-founder of a human resources consulting company. She spends her free time hiking, running, bicycling, and enjoying the great outdoors.

For more information, visit:

http://pamelahutchins.com,

Email:

pamela@pamelahutchins.com.

To receive her e-newsletter for announcements about new releases, click on:

http://eepurl.com/iITR.

SkipJack Publishing:

http://SkipJackPublishing.com/